Preaching to the Choir

The Care and Nurture of the Church Choir

Preaching to the Choir

Wayne L. Wold

Augsburg Fortress
Minneapolis

Preaching to the Choir
The Care and Nurture of the Church Choir
Wayne L. Wold

Editors: Carol Carver and Becky Lowe
Cover art: Markell Studios
Cover design: David Meyer
Interior design: Becky Lowe

Library of Congress Cataloging-in-Publication Data
Wold, Wayne L., 1954–
Preaching to the choir : the care and nurture of the church choir / Wayne L. Wold.
p. cm.
Includes bibliographical references.
ISBN 0-8066-4675-6 (pbk.)
1. Choirs (Music) 2. Church music. I. Title.
MT88.W63 2003
264'.02—dc21 2003004510

Manufactured in the U.S.A. ISBN 0-8066-4675-6

09 08 07 06 05 04 2 3 4 5 6 7 8 9 10

Contents

Introduction

The Basis for Caring

What unique characters inhabit our choir rooms and choir lofts! They are busy and lazy, experienced and rookie, self-assured and hesitant, expert and clueless. They overlook our flaws and search for them. They sing in our choir because of us and in spite of us. They come out of conviction and out of habit. They strive for God's glory and for self-gratification. They are our soul mates and our enigmas. They are a lot like us and they couldn't be more different.

And in what unique surroundings we find ourselves! We gather in state-of-the-art music suites and church basements, surrounded by Gothic tracery and peeling paint.

We rehearse with pianos that are grand and un-grand, upright and downright rotten. We arrive and depart via well-lit parking lots and walkways, and we feel more secure if we can come and go in a group.

And what unique sounds our choirs make! They sing in Latin and Swahili, German and Chinese, Spanish and English. They swallow, roll, or completely ignore their R's. They render their vowels with elocutionary precision, and they are diphthongally-challenged. They make use of octavos and song sheets, missals and memory. They sing chants and canciónes, motets and responses, masses and estribillos, cantatas and specials, chorales and spirituals. They produce heavenly, transcendent euphony and earthy, indigenous cacophony.

And then there are the unique ones who direct these groups! We are under-qualified and over-qualified, over-paid, barely-paid, and not paid. We got our positions after grueling interviews and auditions, and by raising our hands. We do what we do because we feel called by God, and to earn a paycheck. We spend hours preparing for each rehearsal, and we wing it. We wear a special church persona over our real selves, and our lives are open books. We believe our ministry is of utmost importance, and we wonder why we waste our time. We strive to please God, to please others, to please ourselves.

What all church choir musicians hold most in common just might be our diversity.

Yet, beneath all these vast differences lies a common foundation—a reality so strong and so profound that it transcends all that might seem to divide us. That unifying factor is *response*. We have been given a gift, and it begs acknowledgement. Baptism planted a seed, and it has been steadily growing; it ignited a spark that has been smoldering and glowing in us ever since. Through baptism God forgave us, saved us, marked us, connected us to Christ and to each other, and we just can't be quiet about it. Our abilities to sing, or to learn, or to work hard, or to be a team player were not among those gifts granted at the font. But, along with the rest of our human characteristics, these abilities were granted a new focus, a new calling, a new energy, all at that moment when those wet words were heard and felt. "All things are mine since I am his! How can I keep from singing?" asks Robert Lowry in his hymn of the same name. It's a rhetorical question, of course. "What am I to do? I can't help it!" answers Marlene Dietrich. A gift calls for a response.

Baptism is a force that not only calls but levels. Our choir members may have varying degrees of talent, training, intuition, and dependability, but no one dare deny their equality or their value in God's eyes. When we are granted that rare but transforming glimpse of each other—and ourselves—through God's eyes, we soon realize that our differences are of miniscule importance. Our common salvation is a much greater reality than our individual variances.

Furthermore, that individual gifts are so widely different does not disprove the elevating and leveling properties of baptism—it supports it. Just as we cannot all be sopranos, altos, tenors, or basses, so we cannot all be directors, accompanists, or soloists—or even singers, for that matter. Good order requires a division of duties and roles. Good order honors God, proclaims the gospel, and edifies people. Good order shows respect for another's baptism.

I hope you catch the irony in the title of this book. The phrase *preaching to the choir* is invoked when someone is trying to claim that time and energy is being wasted on a group that is already on board. "Better to focus elsewhere" is the implication. While this tactic may be true in many arenas—such as some political campaigns—this is not the paradigm for the baptized. Choir members, as human individuals, are always deserving of love and concern, and there will always be more that can be learned, experienced, and contemplated living under the reign of God. Just as choir robes don't make us any more perfect, they also don't make us any less needy or less deserving than others. Joined together into a choir, we are individually and collectively caretakers for each other and for all God's people in that place. We are spiritual leaders to those whom God has mysteriously called into this specific relationship. Such a high calling dare not be ignored or even treated lightly.

An intense vocational awareness is our wish for all the baptized. We seek it for ourselves, we wish it for each and every person, and we strive to help make it happen for all within our grasp. We can encourage and foster a more profound understanding of God's call—ours and theirs—as we go about our jobs as church musicians. It is often in the *whats* and the *hows* and the *whens* of our regular encounters that we can truly *preach to the choir.*

"Feed my lambs; tend my sheep," Jesus asked of Peter (John 21:15-17). We certainly cannot do the feeding and tending on our own. But God has supplied us with platters overloaded with the grace that comforts, challenges, convinces, and conveys what is needed. And we have been empowered to be *tender* and to be *tenders* for each other. It is an awesome responsibility—but an even more awesome opportunity. Let us explore some ways we directors—in a sense pastors to this flock—might think and act about our calling.

Wayne L. Wold

Chapter One

Planning Ahead Is Pastoral Care

That planning ahead is a good idea should come as a lightning bolt to no one. We would all agree that it is a good idea, do it when we can, and try to make the best of those situations when we did not or could not. But planning ahead is mostly for our own sake, isn't it? We would rather avoid that anxiety, of course, but haven't we learned to cope well enough to get by on a week-to-week basis? Isn't winging it a valuable skill and worthy art in itself?

There are numerous pitfalls to "just getting by" in the planning-ahead department. One is the inherent lack of vision. How can we analyze and adjust our balance of repertoire (see chapter two) unless we can view the bigger, longer-term picture? Some directors plan out (and publicize!) their repertoire an entire year in advance. Others, especially those who have to gauge their repertoire upon a fluctuating number of voices and voicings, find that a few weeks or a single liturgical season is the best they can do. But choosing music on a week-to-week basis is like stamping out fires as they flare up. It can lead us to lose sight of the greater task at hand, and opportunities for better pastoral care are squandered as we jump from one emergency to the next. Neither imbalance in the repertoire nor uneasiness in the choir loft shows pastoral care. Adequate planning is a crucial element of good liturgy, of good relations within the staff, of accountability with our parishioners, of our own well-being, and—our *cantus firmus* here—of caring for our choir members.

The basics

It should go without saying that the primary goal of our planning is to get pieces ready on time. The director must allow adequate time to learn and understand each piece, to develop a teaching plan, to teach it, and for others to actually learn it. (It may also be necessary to allow even more time if we need to acquire the printed music.) We want to introduce each new piece positively and winsomely, to plant the seed of anticipation for the next level of learning it, to build enthusiasm for the end result, and to empower each singer with the skill, knowledge, and security to successfully present it. But that doesn't always happen.

Two extreme examples, related to me by individuals who experienced them first-hand, may help inspire and affirm (or, at least, entertain) you:

> In one instance the director frequently asked the choir to sit quietly during the rehearsal while he studied the music and

determined "how it should go." This often went on for several minutes at a time!

In another setting, a mediator was called in to discuss friction between choir and director. "How much of the rehearsal time should we expect the director to be in the room with us?" asked a choir representative. The mediator was baffled by such a question and wondered what could have been the source of such a question. "How about—*all the time*!" she wanted to say. And just where was that choir director whom the choir members felt should be in the room with them during rehearsals? Either in the next room getting music out of file cabinets or in the church office photocopying music for that very rehearsal!

There—don't you feel better about yourself? But simply staying in the room for the entire rehearsal and choosing music (or copying!) beforehand is still not pastoral enough. Allowing enough time for the director to prepare is only the first step. Sufficient choir preparation time must follow. For many of us, and for most of our careers, adequate time probably meant anywhere from four to six weeks to prepare an average anthem, a few more weeks to rehearse larger works, and just a single rehearsal for most hymns (harmonizations and descants) and liturgical music (verses or antiphons). Such a time frame may still hold true for much of our repertoire. But many of us may not have adjusted our procedures as our musical palettes are widening. Polyphony is a new frontier for those whose past experience was largely homophonic. And monophony, whether singing plainsong or folksong, can be both too simple and too complex for first-time users.

If we are reasonably at home with a healthy smattering of Renaissance and Baroque motets and chorales, Classical and Romantic masses and choruses, later pieces that are modeled after these past eras, and some of the more common sounds and genres of the twentieth century, then many new pieces will have a ring of familiarity about them. They belong to the same stylistic canon; our mind's ear knows what to expect. But the varied repertoire many of us now feel called to bring to our people may need more than this business-as-usual approach. While it is true that music notation is never an exact science, it is even less precise when trying to convey the varied ethnic and non-Western sounds now knocking at the doors of our choir rooms and naves. New styles—even short pieces of a simple texture—need more lead time so their flavor can be caught. This varied repertoire requires more time for the director to study, more time for the learning process, and more time for the singers to discover its message and make it their own.

Many musicians are aware of numerous performance practices when rendering Western music. We know to double-dot the rhythm in pieces which are in the French overture style; we play *notes inegales* at certain points in French Classic literature; we ornament melodies when they return in many works in ABA form. Such indications do not appear on the printed page, often because such practices were so widespread at the time and therefore assumed and also because our notational system cannot convey such subtleties. So we try to become knowledgeable and fluent in any number of these many styles so that we can render them more authentically and more effectively. Our goal is the full and final product rather than just mastering the separate ingredients.

Sometimes even the best-trained and most savvy musicians forget to extend the concept of performance practices to music outside the Western art canon. But music in the various popular styles and that which comes from cultures around the world can also rightfully claim their own performance practices. In many syncopated styles, for example, we may be able to get all the rhythms correct but still fall short of its flavor until we live with it for a while and internalize it.

European hymns are often stylized by shifting into compound meter (4/4 becomes 12/8, for example) in gospel music. Traditional Hispanic music often alternates measures of 6/8 and 3/4, requiring frequent shifting of the accents. These and other stylistic variations can catch even seasoned singers off-guard, making them feel insecure and self-conscious. The quality of worship also suffers when musicians are uncomfortable and provide half-hearted, apologetic leadership. Skill and artistry are built over time through creative repetition and thoughtful reflection.

We honor the musical treasures of the past and present, dignify the individuals and peoples who created them, intensify our worship of God, and provide pastoral care for our people as we plan ahead in our music selections.

Extra-musical basics

As if there weren't enough musical concerns to occupy our time, in the name of pastorally caring for our people there are other details that we will want to be in order. Do any of the following sound familiar?

- You find out right before—or even during—an evening service that the lights will be dimmed, including those above your singers or instrumentalists.
- Two choirs had planned on sitting in and singing from the same location.

▼ Choir members have not been apprised of the procedures for receiving ashes—do we go first? last? by voice part? alphabetically by name? by sins?

Many of our choir members' most upsetting moments are unrelated to the music itself, but they still cast a pall on their choir experience. Anxiety is contagious. Many of these episodes can be avoided by careful envisioning, discussing, and communicating with all concerned parties well in advance.

In all fairness to the directors, many of these unfortunate episodes can come about because of other leaders. Many of us have seen the sign that reads "Failure on your part to plan ahead does *not* constitute an emergency on my part." The statement may be funny, but it's not very often true. Regardless of who is to blame, for the sake of the choir and for good worship we will often need to be buffers and accommodators. Staff tensions should certainly be addressed, but in their proper setting. Rehearsals and services are never those times, and choir members' ears are seldom the appropriate ones for complaints we might have with other staff members. Pastoral leaders know when and how to address problems.

And, despite all our best efforts to plan ahead, the unexpected will regularly make an appearance. Blown breakers and belfry bats, slippery steps and sneezing spells, raucous radiators and redolent robes all seem destined to make an appearance at one time or another. Technology seems to have alleviated some but added even more new opportunities to frustrate us. Being able to think on our feet is crucial at such times, and having a sense of humor can turn a potential tragedy into a favorite memory.

Why bother?

Planning ahead and being proactive about big issues and little details are not just new concerns. Christians often consider the issue when pondering the characters of Mary and Martha, as told in Luke's gospel (10:38-42). Can we, too, become so obsessive about details that we miss the big picture, the *best part*? Certainly. But Jesus was surely not condemning the planners and doers in this story and praising those who go with the flow and live more serendipitously. Rather, he was putting those roles into perspective. Great things seldom take place without careful planning, and good worship should be the greatest of our concerns. After all, good worship is the best pastoral care there is! Perhaps our highest goal is to be good Marthas in our choir rooms and offices so that we can be better Marys in worship.

Planning ahead, as we can, honors God and the baptized, relieves anxiety, builds security and abilities, encourages a better balance, saves time and energy, and allows for worship to do its best work on us. In short—planning ahead is good pastoral care.

Chapter Two

Choosing Music Is Pastoral Care

The previous chapter addressed the *when* and *why* of planning ahead. But here we look more at the *what* and *whys* of choosing what our choir members will find in their folders each week.

There are probably as many methods of choosing a choir's repertoire as there are choirs and directors. Some directors dearly love the process of searching, sorting, and choosing music, and they are energized by it. Finding just the right piece—one that fits the group, the balance of repertoire, and a specific spot in a specific liturgy—is like winning the lottery for these directors. Others dislike the hunting and balancing and acquiring but do it anyway, treating it as a necessary chore. Still others default on this part of their responsibility/opportunity, either sticking with what they already know or grabbing the first new things that come their way each season. The desire for good worship and sensitivity for the choir's well-being call us to be responsible in our task of choosing repertoire.

Sometimes, even when we do put lots of time and thought into our repertoire, we might have a less-than-admirable goal. Perhaps we plan our liturgies so that looking good in the bulletin is the highest priority. ("See how nicely everything correlates?") Sometimes, as John Yarrington has admonished, we plan our services with our colleagues in mind. ("I'm going to an AGO meeting Sunday afternoon, and I want to be able to impress the other members in case I get asked what my choir sang that morning.") Or we choose music to massage our own egos. ("I must be good since my choir can sing Bach.") Or we try to relive our pasts. ("This piece transports me back to my college choir's European tour.") Once again, good worship and good pastoral care may have taken a back seat.

It is really a matter of balance, of course—providing what is wanted *and* what is needed, materials from the file cabinet *and* from the morning mail, that which comforts *and* that which challenges—all for the sake of good worship and good pastoral care. Or, as Bach stated it in the dedication for his *Orgelbüchlein*, "for the glory of God and the edification of humans."

The variables

There are many worship models in the American landscape, between and even within denominations. Repertoire chosen for lectionary-based worship will vary greatly from that chosen without a lectionary in mind (assuming, of course, that the directors in each situation are truly in tune with their parish's tradition). Another variable will be the extent to which the Christian church's historic liturgy is known, understood, and embraced in a particular parish—and to what extent the congregation, clergy, and music leaders concur on this issue.

This diversity of philosophies towards worship is often the catalyst for some of the fiercest battles within parishes and staffs. It is not a new phenomenon, of course; but knowing that does not make our battles any less bothersome. Even though there is—and probably always will be—great diversity on the worship landscape, what we should hold in common is our concern that worship and worshipers be treated with great care and respect.

The many opportunities for choral leadership

Watch out for the *anthem trap.* By this I am referring to the habit of always singing a special choir piece in the same spot at every service—and often little else. Having a set spot for the choir anthem in a liturgical service makes it seem like a time-out or a seventh-inning stretch before getting back to the *real* liturgy. Even in a less structured worship order, the anthem seems to function as just the next item on the program of a religious variety show. Where the anthem trap exists, choir members often see their role as providing just that one piece. They may ask, Why sit together at all? Why not leave once we're done with our performance? Keeping a choir busy throughout a service gives them a better sense of responsibility, ownership, and vocation. It's good liturgy, and it's good human dynamics. What might a choir sing in addition to, or even in place of, an anthem?

Hymns

The choir can lead the congregation with voices alone or with other accompaniment, singing the first stanzas of unfamiliar tunes to help teach them, or singing some stanzas alone in alternation with the full congregation. The choir can provide harmony, embellish with descants, or sing entire hymn arrangements also known as *concertatos* (being cautious, however, not to usurp the hymn from its primary owner—the congregation).

Choir propers

Singing the verses, offertories, and communion antiphons (depending upon the liturgical tradition) that change week by week is a historic role for the choir.

The Ordinary of the Mass

On occasion, the choir may sing one or more liturgical canticles, drawing upon the numerous settings of the Kyrie, Gloria, Credo, Sanctus-Benedictus, and Agnus Dei of all eras and musical styles and voicings, either as choir-alone pieces or choir-enhanced congregational settings. Though it is good theology that congregational singing of these portions of the liturgy be the norm, having the choir occasionally sing specially-composed and specially-prepared settings on the congregation's behalf has much to commend it.

Psalmody

The choir could lead the assigned psalm for the day, either in a choir-alone or in a choir-congregation setting.

Scripture motets

Many compositions are available that set to music one of the assigned readings. By presenting such a work, the choir takes an active role in the proclamation of the word.

Musical offerings

The offering is already a popular spot for the anthem. Though it is open for misinterpretation as a performance or to help pass the time and cover the noises of taking up the collection, choral music at this point is still very appropriate. The musical presentation is an offering of *our selves, our time, and our possessions*: the skills and efforts that have gone into the writing, composing, publishing, finding, purchasing, rehearsing, rendering, listening, and offering all this back to its Source.

Communion meditations

The choir can present music not just to fill the time and cover the noises, but rather to preach and interpret the reality of *God with us* in the eucharist.

Preludes

Before the liturgy, choral music can function in the same way as an instrumental prelude: it can turn our thoughts toward worship, be an act of worship in itself, or introduce tunes and important themes that will be encountered during the next hour.

Postludes

Though not feasible in some parishes due to physical layouts or liturgical practices, an occasional acclamation from the choir at this point may effectively interpret the sending-forth message in a new and powerful way.

Cantatas

Originally developed for liturgical use, later developments in the genre and in worship practices have made it more difficult to use cantatas at an average Sunday morning worship service. Though we might more likely present a choir cantata at a special service or a concert, there certainly are instances where a well-chosen and well-rendered cantata will enhance a service without upsetting the proper balance between word and sacrament, choir and congregational participation.

Other opportunities

Surely our diverse congregations with their numerous worship styles will find even more ways to make good use of the choir, in ways that still keep worship at the center.

Some choirs are well acquainted with the list above, and they approach each liturgy with an open mind and a sense of anticipation. Members from such a situation will be less likely to ask, "What's our anthem this week?" and more likely to ask, "What roles do we take this week?" It is not desirable for even the best choirs to do every possible task at every service, of course. That is not good liturgy or good care for choir or congregation. Balancing their duties, preparing them for their duties, introducing them to new duties, and helping them to understand and appreciate their contributions all call for our greatest care.

Being realistic

While optimism is admirable and encouraged, we must keep our goals rooted in reality. Reading sessions, conferences, and even short workshops are looked upon with suspicion in some parishes. "Do you remember all the ideas he brought back last summer?" goes the conversation around the church office copier. "Drove us all crazy until he finally acknowledged that we aren't that big suburban church that wowed him. Then he disdained us because we weren't, and then he moped around for a few more weeks because he felt stifled here. It's been only a few weeks since he really started doing effective work here again, and now we are being asked to pay for this to happen again this summer?"

It's not that we should avoid mountain-top experiences—indeed, they are also vital (see chapter eight). But we must, for the sake of ourselves and those we serve, keep our goals appropriate. Your choir will not sound as thrilling as when a hundred choir directors sang the same piece last summer. Get over it. If you left off in the spring doing predominantly two-part music, don't expect a fully-balanced, four-part choir at the first rehearsal in the fall, no matter how determined and optimistic you are.

Repertoire has the potential for being a morale-booster or a morale-burster. Some directors feel that only SATB music is worth doing (or worthy of themselves). One choir member related to me at a workshop that her choir wasn't a "real choir." I protested and asked why she felt that way. "We can't do real choir music," she continued apologetically. "We always have to re-write some parts and leave others out. We can never just pick up a piece and sing it as it is written." How sad that this director was wasting their time rearranging and mutilating the printed music, robbing them of their self-esteem, and zapping their joy. What a boost and affirmation it would have been for them to work on a two- or three-part piece, and then be able to do it as written!

Know your group! If you are new to your position, spend time studying the files and the past few years' bulletins so you know more of their history. Look for areas for growth, but not before you identify their tradition, their comfort zone, their gifts. Search out the quality music that does fit your group—it's there. Or create it. Find the gifts that you and your people *do* have and capitalize on them. You are unique—stop trying to be someone else. Otherwise, in the end, you won't be any good at being yourself *or* someone else. Run a reality check—often!

Caring enough to grow

Being realistic is not the same as settling for the status quo. Yes, find repertoire that is attainable. But keep raising the bar so that singers, individually and collectively, will over time improve their voices and musical skills, widen their cultural and spiritual horizons, deepen their faith, and become even better worship leaders. Wanting our choir members to grow and then providing the environment and means for that growth is pastoral care at its finest. In what areas might we find the opportunity to encourage and enable growth?

Musical complexity

The ability to sing harmony, polyphony, or even a good unison are all skills our singers (and the director!) had to master at some point in their lives. Perhaps some are just learning these now. Once we jump over each hurdle we tend to forget what it was like on the other side. Perhaps even more challenging for some of our singers are all those *new* rhythms we find as we discover a wider palette of musical styles. The more grounded we are at the basic musical elements of rhythm, harmony, melody, dynamics, pronunciation, and diction, the quicker we will be able to grasp new pieces and new styles.

Aesthetic refinement

While we want to avoid worshiping and flaunting our "superior taste," we must admit that it is natural for artists to reach towards a level of greater artistic refinement and grow more impatient with those things that display a lower or even nonexistent artistic level. But we must also confess that, to many in the arts, refining one's outlook means limiting to a dangerously small and ever-narrowing set of criteria. True artists find something artistic wherever they look, and they keep looking for more! As artistic leaders, we can encourage our choirs' and congregations' artistic outlook to grow in breadth rather than to constrict into narrowness.

Wider topics

If your congregation has been singing some of the hymns in new hymnals and supplements, you already know what hymnwriters are writing about these days. Did singing about "athlete and band" and "loud-boiling test tubes" ("Earth and All Stars" by Herb Brokering) in the 1970s prepare us for "Woman in the Night" (Brian Wren), or "Mothering God, You Gave Me Birth" (Jean Janzen), or "When the Poor Ones Who Have Nothing Share with Strangers" (J. A. Olivar) in more recent years? New times, new world situations, new awarenesses call for new language. The human voice is the only instrument capable of conveying melody and words at the same time. We want both to bear creative praise to its creator and convey important messages to our co-creatures. We may have many file drawers full of fine settings of "Worship the Lord in the Beauty of Holiness" or "Lord, Hear My Prayer," and these are important, worthy messages. But caring for our people calls us to keep searching for ways to tell the old, old story in new, vigorous ways.

Diversity

Surely this is a key word for the modern church, and no passing fad! Why might we want to expand our repertoire to include more ethnic or ecumenical styles? Because there are persons of that background in our neighborhood and we want to attract them into our parish? Maybe. Because we already have members of a minority group in our congregation and we want them to feel welcome? A good reason to make up for lost time. How about if we have *no* group different from our own anywhere even close to our parish? Does that let us off the hook? No way! Perhaps that is the most compelling reason to expand our stylistic repertoire. We can become so insulated, so parochial, so ingrown, so self-gratifying, that we fail to recognize the diversity of God and God's creation. Adopting—or even attempting—new styles and sounds, new harmonies and languages, proclaims a larger God and expands our concept of God's people.

Language use

We may poke fun at awkward and unsuccessful attempts to be more inclusive and respectful in our language and practices, but the basis of these attempts is the very gospel itself. In some parishes, concern for inclusive language has rendered entire choral libraries obsolete. In other places the issue is ignored completely, and in others its adherents ridiculed. Biased language reinforces the faulty and dangerous message that the gospel message is *not* meant for people of all races, social classes, human conditions, and genders. And using exclusively male pronouns and metaphors for God reinforces stereotypes that are biblically inaccurate and emotionally troublesome.

How do we settle on a policy of language use in our parish or even with our choir? Take a vote and let the majority rule? Probably not. Leaders must lead and advocate. Each situation will call for a different solution, but all institutions can do something helpful. And, should we need to clean up our language—due either to our own convictions or being forced to do so—what do we do with all our existing materials? It is much easier and more convincing to simply choose texts that avoid (or at least minimize) language we are trying to move away from. Many old chestnuts deserve to be phased out by a healthier, more-vigorous strain, and making changes to existing, well-known texts often causes more negative than positive reactions. Inclusive texts that are the most successful do their job without calling attention to themselves. You will find many among the newer publications and, surprisingly, even among the old ones. Talk to people who feel strongly about this and read what they have written. Believe them when they say that words hurt worse than sticks and stones. Inclusive language is pastoral care.

An eye for balance

Keep a well-balanced folder. At any given time throughout the choir year, check to see if there is at least some variety and diversity of musical and poetic style, degree of difficulty, cultural origin, language and images, and overall effect in the current lesson-plan. But, even with all this emphasis on diversity, remember that developing and expanding the choir's repertoire is *not* the ultimate goal. We grow in musical technique, in diversity of styles, in mastery, in liturgical effectiveness, *all* for the sake of worshiping God and serving God's people.

I recall a rehearsal many years ago when, after I handed out a new octavo, one choir member asked, "Didn't we sing this three years ago?" I was so pleased. "Why, yes!" I responded, beaming with pleasure over her accurate memory, her awareness of the three-year lectionary, and of her (obviously) excellent director who so wisely chose this piece to complement the gospel reading. "Then I guess this means we're not getting any better," she concluded.

That was one of the quickest deflations I'd ever experienced. Her primary concern was a worthy one—repertoire was to improve and advance the musical skills of the choir. And my primary concern was also good—repertoire was to serve in a particular place in a particular liturgy. But that conversation does remind us that our repertoire does fill many different purposes to many different people—to us, to the individual singers, and to the congregation. And we seldom have the same set of priorities. Keep learning, teaching, and balancing.

Finding the riches

Caring directors will always be on the lookout for suitable repertoire, and they will look to numerous sources. Following is the beginning of a list.

- Your church's file cabinets While this may sound silly, return to these often. It's a good way to balance the familiar with the new. Even if the choir's make-up has changed since most of the music was purchased, even if a there is a different worship style in place, even if you have a different vision for the choir's role, try to use some things from the archives. It's not only good stewardship, it's affirming and comforting. It's a sign that you are still learning and discovering.

- Your colleagues' filing cabinets Borrowing (or even better, exchanging) ideas and actual pieces of music can create good will between denominations, parishes, and individuals. Friends and peers tend to recommend their best stuff.

- Hymn collections Keep numerous hymnals and supplements on your shelves. Though we can become overwhelmed by the immense amounts of materials during this ongoing hymn and hymnal explosion, at no other time in history has so much substantial material been available to study and to use as hymns or choral pieces.

- Reading sessions Much will depend upon the sponsoring organization. Denominational organizations (such as the Association of Lutheran Church Musicians, Presbyterian Association of Musicians, and Association of Anglican Musicians) and non-denominational organizations (such as Choristers Guild, American Guild of Organists, and American Choral Directors Association) often present these. Those sponsored by publishers and/or vendors will understandably be biased toward their own material, but they will usually be more generous with complimentary copies.

- **Subscriptions** These will usually come from the publishers, so expect to sift through a wide variety of material as you search. The recordings that often accompany these packets are a mixed blessing. The choir on the recording will sound either much better or much worse than your own, and a slick rendition may keep you from noticing inherent weaknesses in the composition. But a recording may also be a time saver, allowing you to search for material while doing something else (such as driving).

- **Repertoire lists** Many journals contain lists of suggested choral pieces. Seasonal and lectionary-based lists are especially helpful.

- **Reviews** These are found in many journals, as well. The most helpful ones are those that describe aspects of the piece such as voicing and degree of difficulty in addition to giving ratings.

- **Music stores** Some have little or nothing on display; others are treasure-troves. They understandably promote the newly-published pieces most heavily, but check the older files and bargain bins. Don't fall into the *top ten* mentality.

- **Write your own** Many potential composers never give it a try. Perhaps they feel it must be either a big production number or nothing at all. Start with smaller genres such as psalm refrains, verses and offertories, hymn stanza harmonizations and descants. Maybe you'll work up to the anthems and cantatas, or maybe you'll decide that the smaller, more modest genres suit you, your choir, and your skills better.

Choosing well is its own reward

Our goal in all this searching is to find repertoire that fits. It should fit our group in number of parts and degree of difficulty, and it should push at their growing edge. It should be worth their valuable time, musically and spiritually. It should fit a particular place in a particular liturgy. Sometimes the director will be the only one who knows all that went into choosing a particular piece and notices why it is just right. But our people do catch on. Amid all the generic cards and musical mugs (ah, the mugs!), you do eventually get one that says, "You make a difference in this world—all the time and effort and caring you give so freely doesn't go unnoticed." Knowing you care builds respect and trust. And choirs who trust their director are the ones who will be most open to new ideas and continue to grow in depth and breadth.

The human mind has an amazing capability to process new information and to keep expanding its database. We want our choirs to do more than get the notes right. We want passion. We want to express emotions and truths that are universal—and our very own. We want to transcend the mundane, and know that the transcendent is right here in the mundane. We really do crave greater knowledge, deeper awareness, stronger solidarity, closer intimacy. But we don't always know that about ourselves.

And we seldom know when such numinous gifts will be given to us, and from where they will come. It just might be in that odd-sounding choir anthem or that foreign-sounding hymn. Maybe we really need a few maracas to shake loose some seeds of thought in our heads; or a tambourine to loosen our limbs to the rhythm of joyous living; or some dissonance to remind us that life is not easy; or some objective counterpoint to make us confront our own self-centeredness; or some strange, new metaphor to expose and confront our prejudices and xenophobia and then help us move from rejection of the other to affirmation. Our comfort zones can and should expand to embrace our discomfort zones. And there we will find—in even greater measure—the Comforter.

Chapter Three

Good Rehearsals Are Pastoral Care

A successful rehearsal is one that, of course, gets the needed work done. But just as important a goal is the choir's sense of satisfaction and accomplishment. They can leave drained or pumped, secure or tentative in their parts, dreading or anticipating the upcoming service or concert, wishing they had skipped or glad they came. Retention is only one reason to be concerned about members' sense of satisfaction. Our sense of pastoral care calls us to be concerned for their well-being and growth, and then we strive to accomplish it.

Rehearsals should be neither undisciplined nor overly rigid; leadership should be neither weak nor authoritarian;

we should neither defer to nor ignore the most opinionated and outspoken members. That baptism has put us all on an equal footing should be reflected in our respectful treatment of each other. But, as pointed out previously, baptism also manifests itself by placing some in leadership positions. We directors honor that calling by being good leaders. "Leaders lead" is the simple yet profound slogan that should go with us into every music rehearsal (as well as every staff, committee, and council meeting). A few years ago, Robert W. Hovda authored a book with the inspired and inspiring title *Strong, Loving and Wise: Presiding in Worship*. He wrote it for and about priests, to be sure, but these attributes are just as appropriate for music leaders.

If we do our advance planning and choose our music well (see previous chapters), good rehearsals are more likely to happen. If these basic elements are not done well, on the other hand, our rehearsals will have many more obstacles to overcome. No amount of excuses, piety, hype, or flattery will quite make up for it. These chapters are in this order intentionally!

Of primary importance at every good rehearsal is pacing. Opening rites may include devotions (see chapter five), something educational (see chapter four), and vocal warm-ups (see Resource List). But once the music-making is underway, a basic outline is to begin with pieces that are fairly well-known to the choir and perhaps of a livelier nature. This leads well into the second portion of the rehearsal where newer pieces are tackled, where the grunt work and woodshedding is done. And, in true ABA form, the final portion of the rehearsal usually returns to pieces that are less demanding and/or better known. Other variants are certainly viable, too, and we will want and need to vary our routine from time to time. Whatever our preferred order and personal style, we must keep an eye on more than just our own goals. And we should run our rehearsals with more than just an eye to the singers' experience. It takes an ear to carefully listen to what they say and sing and a mouth to communicate clearly and helpfully. And it takes a mind to process it all and a heart to make it all come together.

More than a dozen years ago I was asked to write an article entitled "Ten things not to say at choir rehearsal." It was an enriching experience to explore and reflect upon the topic at that time, and it has been great fun to return to it many gray hairs later. The youngster had some good points to make, and the oldster has made only a few revisions and additions to the original. Here, in the quest for good rehearsals, are:

Eleven things not to say at choir rehearsal*

#1 "The clock says it's time to begin rehearsal, but let's wait until more members arrive."

Unless there is a known reason for people to be late (icy roads or a presidential parade, for example), rehearsals should begin on time. The folks that arrive on time are the ones who deserve the break, after all, not the late-comers. Even if the ranks are sparse—begin! That will show the on-timers that you appreciate their presence and ability to arrive on time. Late-comers will feel that they missed something, and they have (though we certainly want to be understanding of the late-comers' reasons for being late). By following the start-on-time rule, the prompt ones are affirmed and habitual late-comers may be induced to try harder. Such a practice shows respect for choir members' time and for the task at hand. Waiting for more folks to arrive is a habit that can only degenerate into a continually worsening situation.

What to say instead? "It's time to begin, so we shall. Thank you for being on time."

*originally in *Journal of Church Music,* March 1988

#2 "Let's use the hymns to warm up tonight."
This usually means, "I don't have any warm-ups planned, and I have heard that choirs should practice the hymns, so we'll combine the two tasks and be done with them." This is not to say that hymns cannot be used in some way to warm-up and exercise voices. On the contrary, using material at hand for some custom-made vocalizes is commendable. However, merely singing through hymns, even in parts, seldom results in a very complete warm-up. Developing singing technique is an aspect of pastoral care and should be rigorously pursued. But, if simply singing or humming through music were an effective warm-up, then we would never need to use real warm-ups at all! If we use warm-ups that truly prepare the vocal mechanism, improve breathing, stretch range, focus tone, improve diction, and fine-tune the ear, then we will realize that just singing or humming through a hymn won't suffice.

What to say instead? "Let's do some vocal warm-ups before we work on the hymns for Sunday."

#3 "Let's run over the hymns for Sunday."
This is related to the previous statement, but it has a different emphasis. Statement two shows neglect and misuse of the warm-up process. Statement three is an insult to hymns and hymn-singing. "Running over" is painfully accurate in many cases. We run over hymns as if with a bulldozer! Leading congregational song is an important duty of the choir, we say. But by neglecting or even mutilating hymns in our rehearsals we only confirm the notion that the choir's anthem is primary and all else is of lesser importance.

Hymn singing seems easy, but it is not easy to be effective hymn leaders. Even if every choir member can sight-read every line, improvement can usually be made in diction, phrasing, stylistic interpretation, and overall leadership skills. By working on hymn-singing the choir gains not only musical skills but also appreciation for the hymn as an art form, as a proclaimer of God's word, and as an act of worship.

What to say instead? "Let's do some work on Sunday's hymns. This entrance hymn needs to be especially energetic, and its message deserves to be heard."

#4 *"Let's sing through this new piece to see what it sounds like."*

As the director you should know what it sounds like! Didn't you choose, schedule, and even plan how to introduce it? If you cannot gain a sufficient understanding of a piece by studying it, then play it, sing it, listen to recordings, go to reading sessions. This is important pre-rehearsal work for the director, and the choir should not be expected to do this for you. Your time together is too valuable to waste.

What to say instead? "Here is a new piece I discovered. Let's sing it and you'll know why I am so enthused about it."

#5 *"OK, that was good. Now, do it again."*

If it was good, why should they do it again? Go on to something else if it truly was good. Or, if there was something wrong, call attention to it and fix it. Don't rehearse your mistakes. Or, if you feel one more run-through would be beneficial just to gain more security, then be clear about your reason. Repetition is necessary, of course, but it can be tedious if not done creatively. The director must respect the singers' time and be obvious about it.

What to say instead (presuming there were no mistakes)? "That was good, but I sense some insecurity. Let's run it again, and this time trust yourselves more." (Occasionally you might get away with "That was so good I just want to hear it again," but don't push *that* button too often!)

#6 "We need to do better on measure 57. So let's start at the beginning."

What will happen? By the time we get to measure 57 most singers (and perhaps even the director) will have forgotten what they were supposed to do and where. If there is something wrong in measure 57, fix measure 57! Isolate what is wrong, work on it, put it back into the larger phrase, and finally into the entire piece.

What to say instead? "There, we fixed measure 57. Now let's back up a few measures and sing that whole phrase, and the next time we sing this piece measure 57 will be as good as the rest."

#7 "I want you to sing loudly at m. 17, softly at m. 23, energetically at m. 34, and smoothly to the end."

Even if singers faithfully mark each instruction you call out, you will probably never get the response you want. Why? Because marks on a page cannot convey enough *sound* information; and we directors should be grateful for that or we could be replaced by a pack of pencils! Don't spend so much time telling what you want—conduct it! By your effective conducting and/or playing, those dynamics and ritards that you want will be made known to your singers, and much more effectively so than with dozens of written instructions. Some have proposed that conducting can be so finely-honed that words never need be uttered. Most of us fall short of that high a degree of accomplishment, but we all are capable of saying more with less.

What to say instead? "_______________!"

#8 "Since we have so much to work on tonight we will not be taking a break."

Without a doubt, rehearsals must be treated primarily as work sessions. But we should also foster other worthy goals, such as socializing. People who know each other better tend to sing together better. And this goes for the director, as well; this is no time to stay at the piano or podium or retreat into the office. Breaks need not and should not be long, but even ten minutes is long enough for folks to get something to drink, to use the rest room (inconspicuously, rather than having to leave the rehearsal to do so), to speak to someone about a personal matter, to walk around and stretch, to recharge. Taking some time out from rehearsal can actually end up being a time-saver; you might be able to accomplish more with a break than without it. Rehearsal, fellowship, and refreshment are not conflicting tasks, and they will enhance each other if we allow them.

What to say instead? "We've had a heavy rehearsal so far and more is yet to come. So please use our six-minute-fourteen-second break as a reward time to stretch your legs, get a drink, and fuel up for the remainder of the rehearsal."

#9 *"I put an announcement in the bulletin that we need more choir members, but it looks as though nobody came."*

So what about those who are sitting right there in front of you? The ones who did come! Don't ignore or take them for granted. Choir recruitment is often a difficult topic, but we should keep the following in mind.

Written announcements seldom get results; personal invitations fare much better, but the strongest draw is the group itself. The sound of their music, the sight of their leadership in worship, the awareness of their commitment and camaraderie—these are the best recruitment. Announcements should be used, of course, especially to let people know that they are welcome to join and how they might go about doing it.

Make sure your choir rehearsals are always listed on all church calendars and weekly schedules. Potential members can appear in our pews at any time, so each and every bulletin should be thought of as someone's introduction to the parish. It is also worthwhile to list choir rehearsals in order to keep that fact in front of everyone in the congregation. This might help to forestall events being scheduled on top of regular rehearsals—or even in our space. Parishioners (and sometimes pastors and councils) often forget how much time we really do spend on our task. Advertise your ministry both in print and in presence.

Keep the tone positive in all recruitment materials. Begging in any form demeans the choir, its current members, and its role. And don't complain to the choir about the lack of new people. These are the ones that are participating, after all; talk of needing new members implies that they are unimportant.

Don't be courting members simply on the basis of their voice and your current needs. You may not need an additional alto right now, but that might change in the future. And remember that a good attitude and sense of commitment are extremely important. The absence of those attributes can make even the finest voice sound sour to our ears.

What to say instead? "I want all of you to be on the lookout for any new choir members. If we had even one more on each part there wouldn't be as much pressure on you to carry the whole load."

#10 "Before going home, let's go to the choir loft as usual and run over the music for Sunday."

(This assumes that you have a choir room that is separate from the worship space.) As stated before, "running over" is often what happens when we aren't careful. A final run-through has many potential strikes against it. If it always takes place at the end of the rehearsal, singers are tired, know they will soon be leaving, and may have already begun to disengage. If the choir loft is some distance from the rehearsal area, they will arrive at different times, some may be out of breath, and some may take a detour to the parking lot. In short, your dress rehearsal may be a step backwards, and members may leave more pessimistic about the upcoming Sunday than if they hadn't sung it that one last time.

The final run-through in the choir loft may just be a bad habit disguised as a tradition. (Churches are very good at collecting these.) If the group is accustomed to singing in both choir room and worship space, they should be accustomed to adapting. If the two spaces differ greatly—in acoustics, layout, or accompanying instrument—then perhaps more of the rehearsal should take place in the worship space. Perhaps the pilgrimage to the loft should take place near the middle of the rehearsal. Or perhaps the rehearsal should make use of both spaces but on an irregular, as-needed basis. In short, use the spaces in ways that are creative, helpful, and pastoral.

What to say instead? "I see no reason why this won't go as well in the choir loft as it did in the choir room, so we will save that for Sunday." Or "I feel we could benefit by working on these next pieces in the choir loft, so let's move the next portion of the rehearsal there. See you there in three minutes."

#11 "It's easy!"

This comment is one I have added to my list after I revisited my original ten. (And, like most of the others, I learned it by negative example—my own!) We probably toss out "It's easy" when we want to be positive and encouraging, but I have come to realize that it may actually have the opposite effect. "This is easy?" they think to themselves. "But I can't get it, so I must not be very good," they might conclude. It is much better to believe them when they say—or otherwise indicate—

that they find something difficult. Agree with them and point out why it is tricky, and then devise a way to solve it.

What to say instead? "Yes, that F-sharp is hard to find since the chord right before it includes an F-natural. Let's hear it again and then sing that chord progression a few times; soon you will master it."

Finally, there are some phrases you really should have in your lexicon.

Offer praise at every possible moment and make your comments specific. ("That tenor entrance was very powerful" rather than just "That was nice.") Even if you can't in all honesty heap praise on them for their tone, diction, or any other musical attribute, find *something* positive to say, even after the most disappointing moments. ("Well, that passage dropped a full step, but at least you kept each chord in tune with itself.") Don't go so overboard that you make exaggerated or false statements, however. ("You are the best choir ever.") Singers will see through such comments, question your sincerity, and come to doubt any and all comments you make. Yes, point out what went wrong and work to fix it. But don't forget about all they did *right*. Say "not quite" rather than "no," "almost" more often than "that was wrong."

And even when it is most difficult to find something praiseworthy to say, you can—and should—say "Thank you!" And it should be spoken *often*. We can always thank them for their presence, which is something not to be taken for granted in a volunteer choir these busy days. We directors don't always know what it is like on the other side of the piano or podium and what it takes to be a loyal choir member some days. We directors don't get to choose whether to attend or skip rehearsals and services. (Ask yourself the question "What did I do the last time I had a Sunday off—one where I had a choice to do what I wanted to do?") But choir members are confronted with that decision nearly every week, and they should receive some positive feedback each time they choose to come.

It's a dicey situation—just who should be thanking whom? I have known directors who felt slighted if choir members did not thank them for all they did for the rehearsal or a performance. After all, this book has been encouraging directors to do even more for the sake of the members. And, looking through lenses of a more cosmic nature, we directors are providing the singers with the means through which they can respond to their baptismal inheritance. That's quite a favor! Maybe we are deserving of their gratitude.

And then there's the service that members provide for each other. "Oh, thank goodness you're here!" exclaims the only tenor, who will now feel more secure and less self-conscious now that an additional comrade has arrived. Yes, there is a symbiotic network of gratitude in a healthy choir, and it should be expressed in words, deeds, and attitudes.

But we directors are in charge of only one of those channels—the one from director to singer. So we make sure we express gratitude for the grace that is shown to us, and we revel in quiet joy when receiving thanks from our singers and when observing the gratitude made manifest in singer-to-singer relationships.

What we say, what we do, and how we go about our saying and doing have enormous impact on their and our sense of satisfaction, accomplishment, and ministry. Much may be beyond our control, but more is within our reach than we know. Caring for our people calls for caring rehearsals. For there we are rehearsing not just singing, but also worshiping, caring, and living as baptized people.

Chapter Four

▼▼▼▼▼▼▼

Teaching Is Pastoral Care

We all might wish for a choir where every member sight-reads perfectly, renders music of every style artistically and authentically, enunciates clearly in any language, makes full use of the vocal mechanism, comprehends the subtleties of liturgy and the church year, understands the choir's roles, possesses great faith, serves with humility, and has mastered the art of personal relationships. But, then, we would have no reason to teach, would we? And we would have no reason to develop ourselves, since the greatest way to learn something is to teach it. How much better it is that our singers are less than perfect, for it gives us the opportunity to encourage and enable growth—in *them* and in *us*. Furthermore, baptism has taken the desire for merely better music and better worship and elevated it to a quest for better people and better praise; baptism transforms our tasks into opportunities, responsibilities into vocation.

It's not a matter of either choosing to teach or choosing not to teach; teaching happens whether we acknowledge it or not. How we go about our planning, choosing, and rehearsing conveys volumes about music, worship, relationships, and faith. And our day-to-day encounters may have a much greater impact than what we say—especially if they are at odds with each other. Words of praise on a Christmas card cannot cancel out a year of non-support. Comments about the honored role of a church choir won't mean much to singers whose choir is under-utilized and under-challenged. Joyous music doesn't ring quite true when sung in a joyless atmosphere. And rehearsals won't command much loyalty when members' time is wasted, or much respect when the music is not really taught there but merely gone over (and over and over . . .).

"Just because you said it doesn't mean you've taught it!" was the philosophy of a well-respected, retired teacher in my community. It's a wonderful saying. But there are plenty of times I wish I had never heard that catchy phrase. Just when I have done my best to gather and organize appropriate information for the classroom, I recall this litmus test and wonder if any of it will truly be *taught*. Remembering this statement often sends me back to the drawing board to evaluate not so much my material as my approach. Our teaching plans should include the *how* and not simply the *what*.

Teaching the music

Learning the pieces at hand (and on the schedule) is a top priority, of course. We want singers to be secure and confident about upcoming pieces both for their own sake and for the sake of good worship. But, even in our smallest and most homogenous groups, singers come to a piece of music with differing degrees of familiarity (either to this specific piece or to its general style) and differing needs for mastering it. Always deferring to the fastest learners will alienate the slower ones; always letting the slowest learners set the pace will irritate the faster ones. Many singers drop out of church choirs because of these frustrations, or, sometimes worse, they stay in choir and bring their finely-tuned aggravation with them each and every week. We must admit that there will never be a perfect number of repetitions. The stronger musicians will just have to tolerate a few extra repetitions at times; the weaker ones will just have to allow the rehearsal to move ahead at times, even when they wish they could hit it once more before moving on. But there are some things we can do to help level the field and find that middle—pastoral—ground.

- **Hold sectional rehearsals.** Work with each voice part separately, or at least separate men and women, so individual vocal lines can be learned without the distraction of other parts. The best sectionals are short and are closely followed by a chance to put those same pieces back together with the other voice parts. Each sectional rehearsal needs its own leader, of course, and this is an excellent way to give your stronger members a chance to take leadership roles. You may even hold auditions for section leaders, and leadership may need to rotate if there are several individuals able and willing to do it. No matter how capable they are, though, giving them specific instructions for their sessions will keep the sessions focused and roles (yours and theirs) clearly defined. Evaluate your sectional system and connect with the leaders often to be sure that tasks are efficiently and pastorally accomplished.

Another pattern, especially useful where there is insufficient space or personnel to hold separate, simultaneous sessions, is to have the director run a single sectional before each main rehearsal. Each voice part then gets a rehearsal every few weeks.

- Introduce some new pieces by sight-reading them. Give each singer the choice to either sing along or just to listen the first time or two. This occupies and affirms the more skillful singers, gives the less experienced singers a chance to hear it before trying it, and gives them all a vision of the finished product. (It may also help the director gauge the time needed to learn it.)

- Offer extra rehearsal time. At the end of rehearsals announce that the official rehearsal is over but that you will remain at the piano for anyone who wants additional help with a problem spot. In my experience some will leave, pleased that their time was respected, and others will stay, some to go over a problem spot, and some just to help out those who wanted one more shot at the upcoming music. (Often, my entire choir stayed for this less-formal rehearsal extension. In reality, we got more practice and the piece was given additional run-throughs. But, because the last few minutes were optional and more like a sing-along, the evening ended on a lighter note.)

- Provide cassette or CD recordings of a new piece or individual voice parts. This allows singers to work on their parts between rehearsals. Check copyrights before making these on your own. (The entire *Messiah* is available commercially with each voice part recorded separately, for example. But warn your singers to use them carefully. I once had a soprano blame me for her speeding ticket. She was so occupied singing "Worthy Is the Lamb" that she was stopped in a 55 MPH zone—going 85! "Driving under the influence of

Handel" is not an acceptable excuse to most highway patrol officers.)

Teaching a little at a time

To be sure, the rehearsal room is not primarily a classroom for music history or liturgy or aesthetics, nor is it primarily a studio for teaching vocal technique, ear training, or terminology. But it is inevitable and even desirable that these topics be a part of our rehearsals. Some of our best teaching can take place in small doses, as sound-bytes scattered around the music-making. And here is where it may reach the most and mean the most, as we make direct connections from what we see on the page in front of us to what we hear in the air around us. Teaching has no ground more fertile than this!

Finding the appropriate teaching tone is important—being esoteric is as uncaring and unhelpful as being condescending. Teach from your own understanding instead of parroting memorized statements, and fess up when you don't know something. Say you'll look into it, then do it.

What might we teach?

- **Begin with the terminology of music.** For example, point out when the musical texture is polyphonic and how all those separate melodies work together to create a unified whole (a sermon in itself on diversity and unity). Or explain that *hemiola* is not a blood disease but rather an example of non-conformity (marching to the beat of a different drummer).

- **Teach development of the vocal mechanism and a singing style that makes the best use of each individual voice.** From warm-ups to final run-through, insist on proper tone, breathing, posture, phonation, and pronunciation. Closely connected are listening skills such as intonation and blend. Refer to leaps by their intervals and you have helped your singers become better readers and listeners for a lifetime, not just better at one particular passage in the piece at hand. Helping singers discover, develop, and use their *voice* (both literally and figuratively) is baptismal theology at its finest.

- **Point out the characteristics of the different musical eras** (Renaissance, Baroque, Classical, Romantic) to help singers differentiate between various styles and improve their ability to catch the appropriate flavor. Musical pieces don't "all sound alike" once we get to know them better.

- **Share some information about the composers and poets.** Many of them led full, interesting, and tragic lives, and some living ones work in some very unique and unusual situations. Or you may know personally the author or composer. Knowing about the people behind the texts and music can bring more meaning to the pieces and relate positively to the singers' own life situations.

- **Talk about your plans for using the pieces.** Even when we plan our liturgies with knowledge and creativity, we may not do as well expressing our vision to our choir. Teach them the basic worship order of gathering-word-meal-sending, of rites involving sprinkling and ashes, of reproaches and ring-shouts, of sequences and shape-notes. This isn't just insider language—it's the language of the church.

The possibilities are endless, but rehearsal time is not. Be sure your small-dose teaching is succinct, beneficial, and pastoral. Teaching is what happens when we care.

Teaching in larger doses

With all the possibilities discussed above, it would be easy to attempt too much teaching during the rehearsal. Rehearsals must be primarily focused on learning and polishing music for the liturgy and, perhaps, concerts. But there are other arenas for education to take place, and some topics seem better suited to settings and formats other than the valuable rehearsal. Schedule classes and other events especially for the choir, but publicize them for the entire congregation. That way your efforts will be made known to the membership and staff, and some of them may even join up.

What might be worth your time and theirs?

The ability to read music is taken for granted by those who can do it, but it is seen as a deep mystery by those who do not. A series of sessions on reading pitches and rhythms can begin to unlock the mystery.

There are many resources that can be used for music-reading classes, or you might be able to construct your own lesson plans. I believe that many systems get the teaching order wrong, at least for singers. More important than knowing letter names of notes is the whole concept of intervals. Connecting the appearance of an interval to its sound makes for much more secure singing. Too much early emphasis on note names also causes people to confuse reading music with perfect pitch. They say, “I can’t read music, because I can’t just look at a note and sing that pitch.” “Neither can I,” I reply. They might be surprised by my response, but they go on to say “But I *can* tell how long to hold a note, whether the next one goes up or down, and about how far.” “Then you can read music!” I tell them. Helping them break the code of reading music, or convincing them they already can, is one of the greatest gifts we can give our singers.

It's a win-win-win situation—benefiting the individual singer, the choir, and the director—and an example of pastoral care in action.

A historical survey of choral music or hymns can be interesting and beneficial to choir members and others in the congregation. Be sure to include lots of opportunities to actually hear the choral pieces and sing the hymns being discussed. It is also worthwhile to coordinate the hymns studied with those sung in worship that week. As with other educational experiences, learning leads to familiarity and greater openness to the new.

Workshops and retreats can be great opportunities for teaching music, improving technique, growing spiritually, and building camaraderie. These might take place right in your usual rehearsal place or at a retreat center, in a two-day overnight format or for a couple hours on Saturday morning. Even if you yourself are an expert on vocal technique or some other related area, your choir still might benefit from having an outside expert lead an extended workshop. In some instances you might swap rooms and/or leaders with another church choir, or you might join with another choir or two for a joint retreat.

Everyone in the parish—from the pulpit to the choir loft to the organ bench to the church office to the pews—could benefit from greater knowledge and deeper reflection on matters of liturgy and worship. Indeed, many of the current tensions, the warped worship practices (in both the traditional and contemporary camps), and the weakened witness that emanate from them are the result of imbalances and misconceptions about what worship is and what it is not. (This is not to minimize the healthy tension that exists in any worthwhile discussion about important matters. It's just that we hardly get to consider the central issues because we are so caught up in the peripherals.)

The basic concepts of good worship all seem so simple and straightforward after hearing them laid out by masterful speakers and writers or worshiping with excellent liturgical leaders. Find some worship and music presentations that are taking place and encourage your leaders, singers, and members to attend. Or organize an event or series yourself. How much better we will be at making decisions when we are better acquainted with the four-part shape of the ecumenical rite, historical and denominational variants, doctrines and pieties, participatory versus exclusionary traits, diversity and inclusiveness in music and language, architecture and environment for worship, worship as proclamation and evangelism, liturgical spirituality, and more.

Congregational leaders—whether called, hired, appointed, elected, or volunteered—are responsible for more than just doing things and making decisions. They are also called by their baptismal anointing to grow into better, more capable leaders. The heart and soul of the church's life is worship. We all need to get better at it.

Whew, that sounds like a lot of work! All that preparing, gathering of materials, and teaching could easily take over our lives and burn us out. No one can or should try to do it all. But the quest for greater knowledge and understanding is not just an activity—it is a mindset, a passion, a paradigm for pastoral care.

Chapter Five

Caring for the Soul

This topic of the soul really should not be addressed separately from the other topics. Humanity has suffered much and missed out on even more on account of the belief that one's body and spirit are of different and even opposing realms. Christianity and other world religions are even more to blame than the secular culture in this severance, as religious leaders have often lauded and encouraged the denial of the body for the (supposed) sake of the soul. But the great truths of creation, incarnation, and redemption all speak to the unity of the physical and the spiritual. Baptism, eucharist, and the proclamation of God's word all enact, consummate, and sanctify the union of the temporal and the eternal.

But, even amid such powerful proofs, we still tend to get it wrong. And we suffer because of it. A body at odds with its mind is imbalanced, even diseased. God instead intends wholeness for creation and each one of its creatures. We are most faithful when we model this ideal in every aspect and activity of life, including worship and its music.

Another reason spirituality should not be emphasized in isolation is that, aware of it or not, we are surrounded by spiritual food at all times and in all places and in all corners of our lives. It's there for the taking. Our eating habits can encourage robust health, or dangerous imbalance, or devastating starvation. This means that our worship planning, our choosing of repertoire, our rehearsals, our teaching, and our addressing problems all have the potential to encourage or discourage healthy, well-balanced spiritual growth. In addressing these many aspects of choir care, we have, in effect, already been considering the soul. So, instead of treating spirituality as an isolated issue, let's think about it as a thread—a big thread—running though all aspects of what we do. Spirituality happens.

The best liturgical, musical, and relational moments are those times when it all comes together—when we catch a glimpse of both the vastness of God and of our own smallness; when we sense the universality of God's salvation yet treasure our personal inheritance; when we feel more alive than ever before, yet, that it "matters not whether we live or die." Why do we settle for the dull and the pedestrian when we are meant for so much more? Because we must learn that there *is* so much more—taught by the Holy Spirit, encouraged by our leaders, and convinced by our own experience and reflection. Musicians seem to have extra insight into the relatedness of the physical, spiritual, and aesthetic, and with this awareness comes responsibility. It's both a blessing and a curse.

"The artist's job," wrote English painter Francis Bacon, "is to deepen the mystery." *Deepen* is a key word here. He did not say *create* it, as some worship leaders seem to be thinking as they occupy themselves creating mood (whether hyped or hushed) or manipulating emotions. We do our best work when we acknowledge that the mystery is present ("bidden or unbidden" wrote Carl Jung), and that we are there to uncover, experience, contemplate, and be transformed by the divinity that is so profoundly present. (See the author's article "On a Role: Thoughts and Perspectives on Our Calling," *Cross Accent: Journal of the Association of Lutheran Church Musicians* 7C [1999], for a discussion of the musician's role as interpreter.)

We want to get beyond learning notes and rhythms and just getting a piece ready for Sunday. We crave experiences that address the realities of life yet transcend them, that are authentic yet beyond our wildest imagination, that are life-affirming yet life-transforming.

This focus is not just for the *unsaved*; the baptized may already be saved but they still need—and deserve—affirmation, renewal, and continuing growth. In fact, baptism is usually the catalyst that triggers the hunger and unlocks the energy to seek more knowledge and gain deeper understanding. We don't want to ignore the potential nourishment that is right there, under our noses, and free for the taking. The phrase *preaching to the choir* is commonly meant to express the sentiment "don't waste your time fixing what isn't broken; focus on the unconverted instead." This interpretation does not apply to the baptized! Salvation is surely not dependent upon our mental or spiritual capacities, but the ransomed soul still longs for greater knowledge and heightened awareness and ecstasy.

"The human soul needs beauty even more than it needs bread," stated novelist D. H. Lawrence. "It is indeed a moral rather than a musical issue," wrote music editor Ralph Vaughan Williams, justifying the expulsion of enervating tunes from *The English Hymnal* of 1906. "Camp," pronounced writer Susan Sontag a few decades ago, "is failed seriousness." We can understand the concepts of beauty versus ugliness, of the tasteful versus the tasteless, of those attempts at seriousness that fail versus those that succeed. But getting even two people to agree in using these attributes can be an exercise in futility. I won't try to apply them here either, but I would like to suggest some ways to help us explore and expand our aesthetic capabilities, strive for the soulful in all we do, and pass on our discoveries to our choirs and congregations.

Exploring the spiritual

When choosing repertoire (see chapter two), in addition to being concerned for its appropriateness to the liturgy and to the musicians' capabilities, we should try to search for soul-music. Life is too short and the message too important to waste on weak and even mediocre materials.

But this does not mean our repertoire must be difficult. The most profound music and poetry have a simplicity about them that exudes integrity and authenticity. Poorly-constructed and quasi-profound pieces are often more difficult in the long run because they resist this naturalness, and it is harder to believe the message they try to convey. And we grow tired of them; just as we master them we realize they have already given us all they have to offer. It may seem that the present era has more bad and mediocre music than any previous time, but it's been there in all eras. History has just not yet had a chance to winnow the grain from the chaff. We may fear suffocating under all the chaff and, rather than risk passing it off as grain, we might ignore new material completely, clinging securely to the proven masterpieces of the past. But it can be invigorating to participate in the winnowing process. Take some risks for the sake of the Spirit and the spiritual. The good stuff makes itself known if we listen with our souls.

Trust your soul's voice, but be sure it uses its ears, too. We bristle when we hear comments that minimize or dismiss completely our carefully—and prayerfully—formed sense of discernment. ("You just have different taste than I do.") Yet, we must remember that, even if our frame of reference is much more well-examined and broadly experienced than others in the parish, we are still products of our backgrounds, of our environments, and, yes, even of our taste. We weren't born knowing even our earliest, most passionate loves, be they Tudor anthems, Spanish canciónes, polyphonic motets, shape-note tunes, country gospel specials, Baroque cantatas, German chorales, African American spirituals, Scandinavian folk songs, Christian pop/rock, twelve-tone masses, or Victorian part-songs. The wider our panorama the greater our understanding; the more we understand the more we have to draw upon. Keep stretching your own expectations and let new discoveries surprise you with their power, truth, and beauty.

Sometimes we find ugliness either disguising itself as the beautiful or hiding in its creases. Search, work, and pray to eliminate sexism, racism, classism, ageism, and any other *ism* from your definition of *beautiful*. Too many church musicians miss out on the thrill and exuberance of soulful congregational singing because they hear it only as a big, bad, messy choir. Too many songs are passed over because they are too old—or too new. Too many spirit-filled world-songs are dismissed because they are deemed incorrect by our checklist of music theory rules. Too many girls' voices are discouraged as the historic boy choirs are idealized over them. Too many ethnic contributions are ignored as we keep our ear channels finely tuned but, oh, so narrow. Too many of our "righteous" objections are just a smoke screen for our ignorance, discomfort, and insecurities, whether conscious or subconscious. Too many of us stifle the Spirit and deny the diversity of God.

Awaken your potential to appreciate more and more; pass it on to your choirs and congregations, and be willing to learn from them, too. Find room for apples *and* oranges in your diet. Add a few more specialty channels to your basic cable package. Expand your circle of beauty.

Sharing the spiritual

Bring those spiritual, musical, aesthetic experiences into the choir rehearsal; don't save them just for Sunday. We directors are often satisfied just fixing individual notes and phrases in rehearsal. We thrive on polishing to perfection each little nuance. We can often omit the complete run-through because the finished product has been playing inside our heads the whole time. But it may be a different matter for many of our choir members. They want, need, and deserve to experience that finished product. Let them have their souls fed.

Kids will often remind me when I've focused too long on details and not enough on giving them return on their investment. "Can't we just sing the whole song once without you stopping us?" a frustrated child will finally plead. Of course. Thank you for bringing me back to the center. Adults are seldom that honest; or perhaps they have stopped even expecting to be fed while they are working. We can be like inquisitive children who take apart a clock to see how it works but are so enamored of each individual component they forget to put it back together, keeping it from working and doing what it was meant to do. Put the musical pieces back together. Pierre Schaeffer resurrects a Pythagorean term—*acousmatic*—to refer to the experience of music's *sound*, detached from the details and circumstances of its production. That's hard for musicians to do! But that's our goal for worship and for every other opportunity that comes our way. It turns a task into a vocation. Share it.

Vocation is when your work, no matter how draining, feeds you. Otherwise it's just a job, or a favor, or a chore, or a drag. Give your singers the ability *and* the opportunity to be fed—frequently. Right there on Thursday nights in the church basement with tired, hard-working saints in jeans and T-shirts and an out-of-tune piano. If the music and words are worthy of both the baptized and the baptizer, they are worth repeating. If they are that good, they need to be heard again and again, for they will keep unfolding truth with each hearing. How much better it is to get lost in wonder, love, and praise than in page turns, second endings, and augmented seconds.

The idea of repeating music for the greater experience might sound like it's in conflict with a comment in a previous chapter about respecting choir members' time and not repeating things unnecessarily. Just how do we rehearse a piece enough to make it our own and get the spiritual bang back from our buck, and yet avoid the boredom which might cause us to miss the music's capabilities to transport us beyond ourselves? *Repetition* is the noun and *creative* is the adjective. Strive for creative ways to repeat pieces and creative ways to use them. Follow the wise advice you probably give your own students and spread the learning out over several weeks rather than cramming right before the piece is needed; it makes for better learning and longer-lasting appreciation. Hearing parts in different combinations (sopranos and tenors, then altos and basses, for example), in varying tempi and dynamics, with text and with a neutral syllable, are all ways to repeat material without actually doing it the same way twice. Repeat creatively. Creatively repeat. Be creative in your repetition.

And why do we think it best if each piece is used in worship only once before handing it back in, not to surface again for a few years? It takes the director quite a few repetitions to appreciate the piece (even before beginning to teach it), and the choir even more repetitions before feeling secure enough to sing it for worship. And *we* are the ones most fluent in the language of music! But most pieces are heard by the congregation only once. It's no wonder most parishioners can't tell a Sweelinck from a Sosa, or a Haydn from a Haugen! (And repetition probably doesn't offend the *other* in attendance at worship either. God knows all the repertoire before it's even written anyway!) This is not a call to sing the same offertory anthem three weeks in a row. But using the same piece as a prelude one week and as a communion meditation later in the same season is not redundant—it's good form and good stewardship. And singers and listeners alike will more likely internalize the message. It's good for the soul.

Finding the spiritual in the routine

It's easy to get lost in learning the music and seeking aesthetic and spiritual experiences and forget what else this choir-thing is all about. The choir itself is a rich metaphor for the church and for the Christian life. We come together; we give up some degree of our individuality (uniform pronunciations, uniform robes) for the sake of the whole; we need and depend upon each other. Each individual voice is unique and complete in itself, yet no one can make harmony alone. Even our own voice is the result of the teamwork of our brain, bones, muscles, and bodily organs. Terms such as harmony, unison, dissonance, consonance, and counterpoint are all terms used in music *and* in describing relationships. Choirs model the leaders-as-servants role, a Christ-like pattern to which we aspire in all aspects of our lives. We pray as we sing and sing as we pray, and we preach good news to each other and to ourselves. We can lift these things up, not to add meaning but to uncover the profound that is there in our midst all along.

Besides the praying and worshiping that goes on as we prepare the hymns and other repertoire for worship, even singers can stop the music and just rely on words for a change. Many choirs have opening and/or closing times for concerns to be shared and prayers to be prayed. The leader might be the director, a designated choir chaplain, a pastor, or one of the members.

There are many devotional resources available for use at rehearsals. Some of these contain just prayers; others include meditations that are topical, seasonal, or related closely to the weekly lectionary. These can help choir members focus on their tasks, understand and appreciate their role more clearly, and relate their preparations to the larger worship experience. Most importantly, they encourage and enable us to pray together, to worship right then and there, and to name that name of the One who has promised to be there, even where just two or three are gathered in that name. Christ has promised to be in our midst, transforming even our messy choir rooms into sacred space, our messy sounds into offerings of praise and prayer.

Discerning the spirit

The Spirit may move where it will, but we need to keep a close eye on the nature of the pieties that we may be encouraging in our parish and in ourselves. Simply put, we can promote either a liturgical piety, which draws its inspiration from and channels its energy back into communal worship, or another type of piety that ignores, turns away from, or even becomes hostile to that central Christian activity. We've probably experienced the latter type, and we might concur with Luther who described the "enthusiasts" of his day as having "swallowed the Holy Spirit—feathers and all!" Many church leaders fear *enthusiastic* pieties for good reason. They can become self-righteous, condescending, and divisive. And then there's the banality and simplistic nature of the music that seems to be inseparable from the movement!

But some of us fear for the wrong reasons. We may resent the extra time and thought it takes to answer tough questions, we may feel our leadership is threatened, we may suspect that our own spirituality is inadequate for the task, we may truly fear the work of the Spirit in our midst. The best way to promote a balanced piety is to provide worship and music that is rich and reverent, contemporary and timeless, and that acknowledges the heart *and* the mind. It is so much easier in places where such a rich tradition is already in place and supported by other worship leaders. But the role of us *spirit-stirrers* is probably even more crucial in those places where liturgical piety is not the tradition.

To be reverent and encourage reverence in others means that we are acknowledging the presence of the holy. It is not an endorsement of the humorless, hushed, or haloed—quite the contrary. Puritanism is just as artificial and lifeless as Pollyannaism. To find humor in something is a sign that we love it deeply and are comfortable with it. It's no coincidence that those folks most involved with the church are the first to find humor in all its dusty corners.

Choir members are usually the best (or worst) at picking up the double entendres in the announcements, the liturgical texts, the sermons, and even the scriptures. (We all have our personal favorites, but those will have to wait for the R-rated version of this book.) Richard Todd, reflecting on Deborah Weisgall's childhood memories of her synagogue choir loft as "a place of soaring voices but also of corny, bawdy jokes," comments, "The comparison might amuse both groups, but one is reminded of the humor at an Irish Catholic wake—in each case, it's the irreverence of a people so easy in their faith that they can afford not to be solemn about it." ("Churchgoing—God for Adults," *Civilization* [October/November 1999]). I'd rather he hadn't used the term *irreverence* (maybe *giddiness* would have been better), but I do like the picture he paints of that spirited choir loft.

Humor—so long as it does not demean or embarrass—can be therapeutic. It's a sign of being alive and an offering of gratitude for being alive. So, the next time you tell your choir in rehearsal to use "birth control" when you mean to say "breath control," or when someone utters any of the ubiquitous comments about the "organ," go ahead and let yourselves enjoy it. God is neither prudish nor prunish, and neither need be the baptized. It's not that the holy is everyday, but that the everyday is holy.

Body and mind and spirit, teaching and learning and nurturing, all go together. We music ministers deal with some pretty powerful stuff. We want to be as awake and aware as we can so we don't mistake the extra-ordinary for the ordinary, the numinous for the nebulous. *Dominus vobiscum! Et cum spiritu tuo!*

Two poems

Hunger (inspired by St. Augustine)

We bless you for the gnawing hunger you have in each soul instilled—
that often-present emptiness that longs, Lord, to be filled.
In vain we scavenge endlessly—our search is never through;
our empty souls are hungry till they find their food in you.

We praise you for the parching dryness deep in every soul entrenched—
that often-present thirstiness that longs, Lord, to be quenched.
In vain we scavenge endlessly—our search is never through;
our wanting souls are thirsty till they find their drink in you.

We laud you for the anxious yearning you for every soul have willed—
that often-present restiveness that longs, Lord, to be stilled.
In vain we scavenge endlessly—our search is never through;
our aching souls are restless till they find their rest in you.

We thank you for the desperate struggle raging deep within each soul—
we offer up our broken-ness and pray to be made whole.
Lord, grant us what we truly need and, by your grace, renew.
We bless you for the energy that drives us, God, to you.

Song at the Well

Jesus, our well,
  thirst you dispel;
  you satisfy every need, once and for all.
Jesus, our well,
  deeply you dwell;
  we praise you and thank you for hearing our call.

Jesus, our river,
  you save and deliver
  from strongholds of slavery to shores of release.
Jesus, our river,
  complete freedom-giver,
  we praise you and thank you for rescue and peace.

Jesus, our spring,
  freshness you bring;
  you send us new water to cleanse and to heal.
Jesus, our spring,
  making us sing,
  we praise you and thank you for grace we can feel.

Jesus, our ocean,
  forever in motion,
  you harbor deep mysteries, you bury the past.
Jesus, our ocean,
  with awe and devotion
  we praise you and thank you for mercy so vast.

Jesus, our rain,
  life you sustain;
  you moisten and soften and cause us to thrive.
Jesus, our rain,
  we are your grain;
  we praise you and thank you for being alive.
Jesus, our water, our life-giving water,
  we praise you and thank you for being alive!

Chapter Six

Interaction Away from the Music

Sometimes the most caring thing we can do is to stop the music. We should switch off the organ or close the piano lid, put the folder and planning sheets away, turn off the lights, and walk down the hallway to that coffee hour, that Bible study, that new member reception, that quilting bee, that seniors' social, that youth group open house. Why might this be important? Take this quick quiz:

- In the classic Disney animated feature *Snow White,* do you remember who is playing the organ? It was Grumpy!

- In the later feature *The Little Mermaid*, do you remember who was the royal music director? It was Sebastian the Crab!

- In the more recent *Beauty and the Beast—Enchanted Christmas* have you heard who is the villain? Is was the evil Pipe Organ!

Either somebody at Disney had a bad experience or we church musicians have some PR work to do! Stereotypes develop where there is not enough familiarity, so we fill in the blanks with our imaginations. We need to be on the lookout for opportunities to become better acquainted with our parishioners (whether choir members or not) and for them to get to know us. We want to fill in those blanks with facts instead of fiction. As we do, we get to know more of these individuals who, though not active in any of our choirs, are important nonetheless. And they realize there is more to us than waving our arms, that we have complete bodies and not just backs, that we wear real clothes and not our albs 24/7, and that we actually have some interests that are not directly related to the liturgy (provided, of course, that we do). We benefit from it, they benefit from it, the community is enriched, and God is praised.

Titles and job descriptions

Granted, many of us do not function exactly the way our official titles read. Based on our own preferences and convictions, we might choose to adopt a slightly different mission statement. But what might some commonly-used terms imply? How might our jobs be viewed differently by choir members, by parishioners, by elected leaders, by clergy, and by ourselves?

In some instances, the musician is called choirmaster and/or organist. Those titles are rather self-explanatory and straightforward and probably very helpful in some situations. In other places, the term may be a variation on director of music ministry. With such a title it would seem that any activity relating to music would come under one's responsibility, including directing, playing, doing programs and concerts, and the ubiquitous and scary *additional tasks* to be named at a later date.

But some other titles are either making a comeback or being newly-minted for the present age, and so are the concepts they imply. Titles that include the term *parish* (parish musician, director of parish music) or *cantor* (meaning director of congregational song or leader of the people's song) are being seen more and more. A different emphasis is implied in these terms. Are we primarily in charge of *supplying* the music (playing the keyboard and directing the choirs), with the hymns and liturgical music secondary matters? Or is our primary focus the entire congregation (of which choirs are subgroupings), helping them *all* to sing the liturgy (rather than just sing *at* the liturgy) and hymns, and using the choirs and instruments in supportive roles?

The point in discussing these varied titles and the inexact science of what they mean is this: To whom are we church musicians responsible? If we are musicians to the whole parish, then we will strive to associate with parishioners, not merely in the hope of recruiting choir members, but because we share a kinship, a camaraderie, a companionship, a pastoral responsibility, a common baptism with them, a desire for their spiritual fulfillment and growth.

Opportunities for interaction

Several possible venues for interaction with parishioners were listed at the beginning of this chapter, and more were suggested in chapter four as possible teaching formats and topics. We might also connect with the parish as a whole through articles in newsletters and bulletins, bulletin boards featuring the music program or special musical events, speaking or presenting in some other way at small group meetings, giving a verbal report at annual meetings, leading informal singing at congregational events, and even giving an occasional stewardship talk or sermon.

We surely don't have to search for opportunities to interact with those parishioners actually in our choirs, but we can look for opportunities to interact in different ways. Sometimes our singers are so accustomed to being just a *voice* that they are surprised when treated as more. I call it the John the Baptist Syndrome, after his reluctance to be known as anything other than "a voice crying in the wilderness." "Hello, I'm an alto," was an introduction I once received upon coming to a new position. I had to ask insistently to get a name! And in one bell choir I directed, a ringer named Effie had been loyally attached to the same couple bells for years. They were, appropriately, the F and E! She stood next to Edie, who probably would have liked to ring bells E and D, but, since Effie already played the E, Edie settled for C and D. Now that's identifying with your musical role!

Directors should resist the temptation to think of our singers (and ringers) as just spaces in our choirs instead of individual persons, or even to imply that attitude through our behavior and comments. We can keep track of absences and ask if everything is all right when we see them again. We can be understanding when they really must be gone. We can ask about health problems and aging relatives and new arrivals. We can keep track of birthdays and mention them in rehearsal, and we can send personal notes (e-mail has made contacting individuals even easier than calls or cards). We can publicly celebrate their choir anniversaries and, especially, retirements (see chapter seven).

In short, interaction outside of the music is all about *being* human, treating *them* as human, and letting them see *us* as human—humans that care.

Chapter Seven

Pastoral Care at the Stress Points

There will undoubtedly be times when the crystal ball will not reveal very clear answers, where it's not just a matter of pastoral care versus un-pastoral care but where worthy ideals are applying pressure on both sides of an issue. The rights of one baptized individual seem to be at odds with the rights of another. I refer here to problem voices, problem attendance, and problem directors.

I had intended to avoid these issues altogether, since I have yet to hear about or create any definitive solutions. But on several occasions, when giving presentations or when discussing this writing project, these topics have quickly and consistently arisen. In many volunteer choirs, they are the defining issues of pastoral care. I had also planned on skipping over these tough topics because *every situation is unique and calls for a unique solution*. Given that, what can be said at all? This statement will be recycled during the course of this discussion and resorted to one final time at the end of this chapter, so there's no reason for the reader to jump ahead to the end to see how it all turns out. There is no mystery in this plot; my comments will keep leading anticlimactically back to this very same conclusion. But let's see where our minds might wander in the meanwhile.

The problem voice

One stressful situation involves choir members whose participation has passed from being beneficial (or at least causing no harm) to being detrimental. (And they're usually the nicest and most loyal people, aren't they?) Age or illness has taken a toll on their ears, eyes, vocal cords, lungs, or reflexes. And it shows. Pitch may have become inaccurate, or the vibrato so wide that the whole concept of accuracy is a moot point; the actual pitch is not really missing—just hard to pinpoint. Tone may have become harsh and does not blend; *bel canto* has become *can belto*. Entrances and cut-offs may still be on standard time while the rest of the choir is on daylight-savings time. And that's putting it nicely!

What would be an easy decision in many musical organizations is made more complicated both by those conflicting voices in the choir ("I won't stay if he does!" "I'll quit, too, if you kick her out!") and by those voices in our own heads ("I must have a good choral sound for the sake of decent worship, for the happiness of other members, and for my own satisfaction." "This individual deserves to be treated with care."). You can't just send a pink slip or opt for non-renewal of contract with volunteer singers—*baptized* volunteer singers.

Most directors and choir members will be understanding for awhile. Maybe, we hope, the situation will work itself out if we wait just one more week . . . or month . . . or year. Sometimes that really does happen. Blessings on those members who excuse themselves when that time comes! And blessings on those who come to their directors and say, "I saw what happened when so-and-so didn't know when to exit; so promise me you will tell me if and when I am no longer beneficial to the choir." (This is no fairy tale! I heard it with my own ears!) But, if a problem stretches on too long, it will take a toll—on membership and attendance, on morale, on effectiveness in worship. You must lead, and you want to lead pastorally. Sometimes it is more caring to tell a singer it is time to retire than to let them stay on. And sometimes not. (Did I mention that *every situation is unique and calls for a unique solution*?)

First of all, don't let this all fall on you! Choir officers can be called upon to help address a present situation or set policies in advance. Even if they take it bitterly, it is much better for them to think it was the choir rather than the director that thought they should leave. Maybe your worship committee is the best arena for the discussion. Pastors can be consulted and perhaps even actively involved in any necessary conversations with the individual. Keep your discussions confidential, professional, and pastoral; don't let it become gossip fodder for the rest.

Following are a few approaches that I have seen help.

▾ Work with the individual and listen to his/her voice by itself (this is more easily handled in those situations where, as a matter of course, the director hears all singers individually every year). It's not just children that have trouble hearing their own voices and matching pitches. A one-on-one session (or two) can actually help solve a life-long impairment. Or perhaps you can determine the nature of the problem, suggest ways to make improvements, or, for bigger problems, recommend a visit to an appropriate medical professional.

- When choir members do retire from the group, throw big celebrations. In addition to honoring them for their service, it may also help other members visualize what glory awaits them when they do the same.

- Some members do quit because they want to leave before they become problematic. When they do, encourage them to include that bit of information when saying farewell to the rest of the choir. It may plant an important seed in the others.

- Some may respond to the stronger approach: "Tell me when you plan to retire from choir and we will throw a huge reception to honor your many years."

- Or you might say, "We are getting handbells and establishing a handbell choir. We will need strong music-readers for this, and I am hoping you will switch from the singing choir to the new handbell choir."

- To a soprano whose tone has become harsh in the higher range one could offer, "I noticed you sometimes strain in the higher register. I could sure use you in the alto section. Would you consider helping us out there?"

- Or suggest other ways they can serve in music ministry. Perhaps they can assist with the music library, folders, vestments, social events, mailings, or phoning. Or perhaps other staff members can suggest tasks in other areas of the parish.

- Surely there are more ways these situations can be prevented, solved, or at least made easier. Talk to colleagues. Pray about it.

Before going on, here is the refrain I promised: *Every situation is unique and calls for a unique solution.*

The attendance problem

Some singers can accomplish in one rehearsal what it takes others six or seven to do. Some can read so well that they would never need to come to rehearsal for that purpose. But, as previous chapters have pointed out, learning notes is not the only benefit of rehearsing together. We grow mentally and spiritually. We help each other with our voices and our presence. We support the church and this small-group ministry called *choir*. So what do we do about members whose attendance patterns are more serious than an occasional miss? What if our excellent repertoire, dynamic rehearsals, winsome personalities, warm camaraderie, and strong sense of purpose are just not quite magnetic enough to keep 'em coming?

Some choirs have attendance polices in place just for this purpose, and it is much better if the policies have been created and adopted by the choir or choir officers rather than by just the director. A policy in many church choirs reads, "If you miss a rehearsal, then you may not sing at the next service." It's a nice, black-and-white type of policy, if that's what you need. It probably works better in larger choirs, and it is more necessary in situations where rehearsals tend to devote most time and energy to the upcoming Sunday's music.

But, in choirs where pieces are worked on several weeks in advance or where re-runs are occasionally utilized, that next Sunday's music might actually be in fine shape. And in smaller choirs, where each individual makes up a larger percentage of the group, just who is being disadvantaged by eliminating that voice? Perhaps it's that one singer, who may have had a perfectly good excuse for being gone. Perhaps it's the rest of the singers, who will miss that support. Perhaps it's the director, who will be disappointed with a sound that is less than it could have been. Perhaps it's the congregation, on account of all of the above.

Maybe another policy is better suited for your situation, such as: "If you miss one rehearsal, you may sing the next Sunday; but show up a bit early to go over the music. If you miss two in a row, you must contact the director who will decide if you should sing or not. If you miss three in a row, assume that you will not sing until you return to rehearsal."

If you and your choir actually look forward to having extra singers during the festival seasons, publicize in newsletters and bulletins that "anyone wishing to sing in the choir for Christmas must attend all rehearsals in December" (or any other deadline you wish to set).

Having no attendance policy or an *anything-goes* attitude undermines the integrity of the group, insults those members who are faithful, reinforces bad habits, and benefits no one. Finding the right balance of legalism, pragmatism, and pastoralism can be challenging. But, when created and administered with careful and care-filled thought, a policy preaches loud and strong to the choir.

Other practices can help us, too. Hang a calendar in the choir room specifically for members to indicate when they plan to be gone, and encourage them at each rehearsal to update it. This practice can help the director in planning music ("What! No tenors on Maundy Thursday! At least I found out a month in advance!"), and it serves as a reminder to the members that their presence is important ("I want to sleep in! But I didn't sign up to be gone today, so I better go.").

We might cringe if we hear a singer in our congregation say, "I won't sing in the choir but will do solos." You might make it a policy that any solos to be sung will be done by choir members. This will show support of your regular choir members, discourage the *prima donna* attitude, and may even encourage a good singer to join the choir.

Above and beyond the appreciation you express at each rehearsal and service, make sure it is done occasionally on a much larger scale. Print the names of all choir members in the bulletin at least once each year. Some parishes celebrate Choir Appreciation Day or Church Music Sunday, which can be a good opportunity for recognition. Sometimes, however, we celebrate choir members by making them work harder than ever at a big service or concert!

Consider a dinner with a program or a speaker. The director may need to be the catalyst to initiate the practice and make some of the arrangements, but this should be sponsored by the congregation (or parish council or worship committee on the congregation's behalf). The people in the pews and congregational leaders need to be reminded of all that our choir members do for the congregation and then do something to express appreciation. Choir dinners also serve to build the group spirit, focus on accomplishments, and encourage socializing in an out-of-the-ordinary setting. In parishes where there is more than one adult choir (and don't forget the bell-ringers and other instrumentalists), these people really may not know each other very well. You might consider handing out certificates of appreciation, presenting awards for anniversary years, honor anyone who is retiring, and maybe even make light-hearted *roasts* (for the most gum under the pew, messiest folder, best excuse for being late . . .).

Finally, we must remember that good planning, good repertoire, good rehearsals, good teaching, and good faith are all parts of the positive choir experience. Short of a Star Trek tractor beam, these are the best means for retaining membership and encouraging regular attendance. But a good policy can't hurt.

Well, here it is again: *Every situation is unique and calls for a unique solution.*

The problem director

Though I believe these problems are much rarer than the ones addressing problem voices or attendance (and the individuals attached to them, of course), they tend to be much more troublesome, cause greater chaos, and produce an even more toxic atmosphere. Since this book is more likely to be read by choir directors than choir members or pastors or church committee members, I address these thoughts to you directors for some self-examination.

Who are problem directors? You tend to be volunteer rather than paid, either because the church is small and has limited resources or because you refuse payment. You do this for the glory of God rather than for the money. That sounds wonderful. But look a little deeper into your own motives and evaluate the situation carefully. Make sure none of the following scenarios are true.

Some people refuse payment for selfish purposes, their pious, public statements notwithstanding. To whom are volunteers responsible? Nobody, really. A pastor cannot force or even expect a volunteer musician to attend a meeting to plan worship. A parish council or personnel committee cannot force a volunteer musician to hold rehearsals that are regular, effective, and pastoral—or even hold them at all! Dissatisfied choir members have little recourse when their director is not bound by any contract, job description, or system of evaluation. You can't be fired if you weren't hired. The terms of employment are *my* terms. Gotcha!

Some people take on leadership positions for psychological reasons. They are needy of attention, power, or authority over others. Or they feel their guilt or spiritual inferiority can only be alleviated by being a super-doer, their Christian vocation fulfilled only by public, highly-visible service. "And I do it all without pay!" says the misguided martyr.

Toxic directors, no matter what their unique chemical make-up, do long-lasting damage to individuals, music and worship programs, and parish life as a whole. Don't do it.

"But I'm not any of the above!" you say. Praise God—and you—if that's true. What's the best way to keep your good situation good?

Treat your position as an appointment. Grow and develop your skills. Develop a job description and insist on periodic evaluations. Work to make the position a paid position, based on standards set by appropriate professional organizations and customized to your setting. If you choose to give back the salary, well and good. But first take that check, deposit it, and write out another one as an offering. We cripple our parishes and our profession by refusing payment, and we build unhealthy dependencies that are hard if not impossible to shake. What happens when volunteer leaders depart? Churches may be surprised to find out that they don't get many applicants for a volunteer position. Budgets not accustomed to having a line entitled *musicians* may have a hard time adding even a minimal amount, and any salary will be considered exorbitant. Any future music leader will be looked upon with derision and their Christian commitment questioned because "they wouldn't do it unless they were paid!" How much better for all concerned if we function as professional leaders, working at being both professional and a leader.

Enough talk about the problems around us? Thought so. Problems are inevitable, but let's try to solve more than we cause.

Oh, one last thing: *Every situation is unique and calls for a unique solution*.

Chapter Eight

Nurturing Your Self Is Pastoral Care

Since keeping a balance seems to be the common theme running throughout these many different aspects of choir nurture, we must not close before getting in a word about nurturing *you*, the director. If we have been stepping primarily outside ourselves in order to be more empathetic toward our singers and to focus upon their overall well-being, we must step back inside ourselves so we can consider the challenging but crucial balancing act that exists here as well. Just as leaders cannot be focused entirely on their own goals and needs, they cannot deny self so much that they do not let themselves be human. Robots may be interesting from an engineering point of view and they may save a lot of work, but we hardly look to them for their creativity. Zombies may pique our curiosity and stimulate our spines, but they are hardly known for their warmth. Humans relate best to those of their own species.

Directors may differ from choir members in duty, responsibility, and authority, but we still have in common with them our humanity. We all are capable of feeling energized and tired, euphoric and depressed, focused and preoccupied, confident and reticent, running on full and running on empty. We deceive no one when we try to deny or override our true natures. Often those around us become aware of our maladies before we ourselves do; we are often the last to realize—and admit—that all is not well. We, too, are a part of that very creation, incarnation, and redemption that we work so hard to convey to those in our choir lofts and pews. We are most effective when we are most ourselves—our baptized selves.

Paul Westermeyer addresses balance for church musicians using metaphors borrowed from the Bible, the kennel, and the front step. He writes:

> To be a servant of all is to carry out one's vocation and office for the sake of all. Self-assertiveness is not necessitated by the drive to boost one's ego. Self-assertiveness is necessitated by servanthood. Precisely because every vocation and office have their contributions to make to the common good, neither lapdog nor bulldog are the right images. Servanthood is the right image, but that does not mean doormat. Doormat is precluded. Servanthood means self-assertiveness on behalf of the whole people. ("Some Theological Basis for the Self-Assertiveness of the Church Musician," *Cross Accent* 8, no. 1 [2000]: 37)

This emphasis on self is surely not a call for narcissism or complacency. We are to grow and develop, and we do so, not to become less like ourselves, but rather to discover and develop all that we truly are. Just as we base our care of others on their baptismal birthright, so does our own inheritance permit us, call us, even command us to grow and flourish. Just how might we best respond to this rich inheritance? What really is our goal? Our plan of action?

In 1 Chronicles 15 we hear of the pageantry and protocol that surrounded the return of the Ark of the Covenant to Jerusalem. Reading these and related passages are enough to make a *rubricophile* drool! But, compared to all the excruciatingly detailed instructions on other aspects of the celebration, there is a rather terse description of the one who would be in charge of all the music. "Chenaniah, leader of the Levites in music, was to direct the music, for he understood it" (v. 22).

How's that for a job recommendation? This one short phrase—understood it—says it all, thought the chronicler.

How would we like *that* to appear as the lone qualification for our positions—just to *understand*? And what if our job description's list of duties simply said to do *it*. This phrase says so little and yet so much. Just how do we go about identifying the *it* of music ministry? And then how do we go about this quest for *understanding*?

For starters, we develop our musical abilities, both natural and acquired. From those first music lessons, to our classes and musical groups in school and church, to perhaps even advanced study and degrees, we have been encouraged, inspired, cajoled, and even intimidated into drawing out what is inside of us and stuffing in what isn't. Most of us stop learning too soon. Knowing just enough to get by is sometimes all we strive for. We let the mediocrity around us wear us down and set the standards. We let the publishers or the recording industry or popularity polls tell us what music to choose. We must search for better paradigms. We should notice that the greatest individuals in nearly every field are those who never stop learning and never stop thinking for themselves.

In his golden years, when he could have been living in the glow of his well-deserved fame, Haydn discovered in London the charm, beauty, power, and ministry of Handel's oratorios. Haydn had not encountered such a genre before—meant for the general public in their vernacular language and based on important biblical stories, but utilizing the finest art in writing, playing, and singing. Haydn chose a lofty topic—the creation of the world—and experimented with sounds new to his and his culture's ears; he worked to get *The Creation* performed in its original German for German-speaking audiences and quickly translated into English for English-speaking audiences. We can admire Haydn for continuing to learn, for being humble enough to admit he didn't know it all, for getting excited over a new discovery, and for striving to minister to those outside his nationality and religious denomination.

Haydn is not the exception. History teaches us that the greatest individuals are often those who learned, lived, and loved the most. We must not leave our commencements thinking that our degrees are all that we will ever need. Passion for growth will make highly-trained organists attend a workshop in order to understand more of the subtleties of leading congregational song. Experienced instrumentalists will be seen taking percussion lessons from a recent immigrant so their music will capture a greater authenticity. Conductors who can skillfully navigate a choir and orchestra through Stravinsky's *Symphony of Psalms* will attend—and participate in—a Taizé service so they can begin to understand this simple, prayerful, soulful music. And they might just as well be seen attending a session on skills for working with young children, or senior citizens, or people with disabilities.

Church musicians with a passion will search out daylong workshops, weeklong seminars, summer sessions, even full degree programs that might take years to complete. In between they will read journals and books, watch instructional videos, join and participate in professional organizations, and attend services and concerts both like and unlike their personal preferences and experiences. And they will stay musically active themselves, singing or playing in an ensemble under someone else's direction so they keep their own skills alive, continue to develop artistically and aesthetically, and interact with peers. Though they avoid showier and extended pieces in worship, they will occasionally present concerts featuring themselves and their choirs for the sake of community outreach, self-development, and self-fulfillment.

And they don't stop with just the music! Theology, philosophy, sociology, anthropology, psychology, art, literature, dance, languages, gerontology, communication, education, history, gender and ethnic studies, and even the natural sciences have something to share with those who have a passion for worship. More specific topics also may catch their attention. People skills, for example, are among the most crucial in clergy-musician and congregation-musician relationships, but they seldom get much attention in degree programs. Church musicians knowingly nod when they see books and seminars on such topics as "Working with Difficult People" and "How to Motivate Others" and long to improve in those areas.

This can be you! Discover what you're missing, that which would enhance your effectiveness and sense of well-being, then get it!

But don't stop with just accumulating information and experiences. Keep a close eye on yourself. Recognize signs of apathy, burnout, cynicism, and anger, and then address them. Do what it takes to become emotionally healthy. You are that important. It may take some rest or reflection. It may take counseling or medication or some other treatment. It may take a leave of absence or a resignation. It might take something bold and breathtaking to shock us into health.

Shocking is the way we often experience that story found in Mark 5:21-43 of the unnamed woman with a flow of blood that has gone on for twelve years. Her story interrupts the narrative already underway—the story of Jairus and his daughter; it violates the polite tone of our worship; it intrudes on our communal persona with a way-too-personal episode. "Too much information!" we may inwardly protest. "I'm glad that's not me."

An illustration by Gail O'Day, homiletics professor at Candler School of Theology at Emory University, has found its way into several printed and on-line preaching resources ("Do Not Fear, Only Believe," *Pulpit Digest* [July/August 1988]: 330–334), and it brings each one of us—female and male alike—into this story. "What is your flow of blood?" she asks. "What is it that has been draining life out of you for twelve years, fifteen years, twenty-five, thirty years? What is it that you have resigned yourself to, preferring death and dying to the active decisions for life?"

Yes, she's on to something here. "Just tired" doesn't begin to describe the maladies of many church professionals. Stop fooling yourself. Most likely your self is the only one you're fooling—others probably caught on long ago. That woman, known only by her condition, along with Pastor O'Day's soul-piercing exegesis, calls out to us, "Discover what it is that drains you, that saps your strength and zaps your well-being—find it, name it, and get it healed!"

Following is a list of possibilities to get you started.

Professional issues

- ▾ inferiority complex
- ▾ superiority complex
- ▾ serving in a denomination whose teachings or practices conflict with your own
- ▾ serving in a parish whose teachings or practices conflict with your own
- ▾ serving on a staff with dysfunctional members
- ▾ being a dysfunctional staff member
- ▾ insecurity about your abilities or qualifications in some area
- ▾ lack of challenging work to do
- ▾ lack of resources (human and other) to do fulfilling work
- ▾ lack of time to do things well

Personal issues

- ▾ financial stress
- ▾ family stress (spouse, partner, children, extended)
- ▾ sexual orientation (if at odds with self or with others around you)
- ▾ sexual dysfunction
- ▾ guilt (real or imagined)
- ▾ physical disorders (illnesses, conditions)
- ▾ psychological disorders (anxiety, attention deficit, bi-polar, paranoia, or others)
- ▾ anger control issues
- ▾ lack of faith

See anyone you know in this quick list? See yourself? Make this your resolution:

I will discover what it is that drains me, that saps my strength and zaps my well-being—I will find it, name it, claim my birthright, and get healed!

Lest this sound like a superficial answer, we must acknowledge that issues of this magnitude and complexity are seldom easy to encounter. It can be a lifelong quest to discover, come to terms with, and address such major issues. And, even when everything that can be done has been done, we may find we still have to live with some consequences and residue from those unhealthier times. Just as that woman couldn't get her twelve years back to live over, we can't fix our pasts. But healing brings an opportunity much greater than being able to turn back to the past. It opens up a future.

That woman knew where to find healing, and finally, even smack-dab in the middle of someone else's life-changing moment, she had it within her reach. And she did something about it. There's power in that garment's hem! As frequent dwellers in the house of the Lord, as caretakers of the church's liturgy, and as channels of healing to others, we musicians have that hem very close at hand. We see it, sing it, play with it, plan it, hear it, write it, teach it, enact it nearly every day. We continuously draw attention to that hem, and we do what we can to bring that hem to all who need it; in our ministry we are honored to be the channel that brings the grasper and the graspee closer to each other.

Yet, even while we frequently handle such holy things, we often immunize ourselves from receiving the benefit for ourselves. Is it from modesty? Or do we believe we are merely outside spectators? Are we not needy enough to grasp that hem for ourselves? Are we so unworthy that we are beyond help? Using a term coined by Parker J. Palmer, do we practice *functional atheism*? Do we not trust the promises we try so hard to proclaim to others? Get healed. Then live as one who has been healed.

Ultimately, don't forget the grace! The very same grace that demands we treat others with equality, dignity, and charity isn't honestly proclaimed by us until we—ourselves—open and partake of those very same gifts for ourselves.

Oh, taste and see that the Lord is good! Very good! Preach it! Live it!

Afterword

Vocation

"Feed my lambs; tend my sheep," Jesus asked of Peter in John 21. "Feed my sheep," Jesus asks of anyone who would respond to his call. That makes what we do as church musicians not just a job or a hobby but rather a calling—what we have come to call *vocation*. We probably hear that term used frequently and indiscriminately—even in the church. But isn't it just a loftier-sounding word for a *job*? And doesn't having a vocational outlook take more time, more energy, more commitment?

Frederick Buechner begs to differ. He wrote, "Your vocation is the place where your deep gladness and the world's deep hunger meet" *(Wishful Thinking,* 1993*).* Think about all those words he used—common words, but put together in such a way that they say something decidedly uncommon.

The world is indeed a hungry place. But the hunger is often misdiagnosed and its remedies ineffectual. And it runs so deep that our myopic sight is often unaware of it. The church's worship, along with its attendant music, is indeed an opportunity to encounter, address, and—with God's help—alleviate some of humanity's deep hunger. It is a noble calling, and leaders with a strong sense of vocation will undoubtedly be more effective *feeders* in the long run.

But the other half of Buechner's equation deserves our consideration as well. A sustained, energetic ministry is also rooted in our own "deep gladness." That's not the same as having fun, getting warm fuzzies, or feeling affirmed just because we get compliments. A deep gladness is one that is hard to feel at times; in fact, it sometimes feels just like its opposite. But, as gladness continues to run inside us, it will carve an ever deepening channel and, over time, become a wide canyon where even more of that gladness and hunger can meet, interact, and be transformed.

Furthermore, Buechner calls this intersection of deep gladness and deep hunger a "place." A vocation, then, is not found in contracts and job descriptions, or based on numbers or consumer satisfaction, but it is finding that *place*—that *crossroads*—that *cross*—where the vertical and horizontal intersect.

Soli Deo Gloria!

Appendix

Selected Resources for Church Musicians

Following is a selected list of books, periodicals, organizations, and websites that can assist us in our work as church musicians. Some of these books may no longer be in print, but they are listed anyway since they can be found in many libraries and used-book venues.

General resources on worship and music

Best, Harold M. *Music Through the Eyes of Faith*. San Francisco: Harper Collins, 1993.

Blackwell, Albert L. *The Sacred in Music*. Louisville: Westminster John Knox Press, 1999.

Brownstead, Frank, and Pat McCollam. *The Volunteer Choir*. Washington, D.C.: The Pastoral Press, 1987.

Cronin, Deborah K. *O For a Dozen Tongues to Sing: Music Ministry with Small Choirs*. Nashville: Abingdon Press, 1996.

Dawn, Marva J. *A Royal "Waste" of Time: The Splendor of Worshiping God and Being Church for the World.* Grand Rapids: Eerdmans Publishing Company, 1999.

_______. *Reaching Out without Dumbing Down: A Theology of Worship for the Turn-of-the-Century Culture.* Grand Rapids: Eerdmans Publishing Company, 1995.

Doran, Carol, and Thomas H. Troeger. *Trouble at the Table: Gathering the Tribes for Worship*. Nashville: Abingdon Press, 1992.

Foley, Edward, ed. *Worship Music: A Concise Dictionary*. Collegeville: The Liturgical Press, 2000.

Johansson, Calvin M. *Discipling Music Ministry: Twenty-first Century Directions*. Peabody, Mass: Hendrickson Publishers, 1995.

_______. *Music & Ministry: A Biblical Counterpoint*. Peabody, Mass: Hendrickson Publishers, 1984.

Lathrop, Gordon W. *Holy People: A Liturgical Ecclesiology.* Minneapolis: Augsburg Fortress, 1999.

_______. *Holy Things: A Liturgical Theology*. Minneapolis: Augsburg Fortress, 1993.

Myers, Kenneth A. *All God's Children and Blue Suede Shoes: Christians & Popular Culture.* Wheaton: Crossway Books, 1989.

Reagon, Bernice Johnson, ed. *We'll Understand It Better By and By: Pioneering African American Gospel Composers.* Washington and London: Smithsonian Institution Press, 1992.

Routley, Erik. *Church Music and the Christian Faith.* Carol Stream, Ill.: Hope Publishing Company, 1978.

Saliers, Don E. *Worship as Theology: Foretaste of Glory Divine.* Nashville: Abingdon Press, 1994.

Schalk, Carl. *First Person Singular: Reflections on Worship, Liturgy, and Children.* St. Louis: MorningStar Music Publishers, 1998.

________. *Luther on Music: Paradigms of Praise.* St. Louis: Concordia Publishing House, 1988.

Schattauer, Thomas H., ed. *Inside Out: Worship in an Age of Mission.* Minneapolis: Augsburg Fortress, 1999.

Spencer, Jon Michael. *Protest & Praise: Sacred Music of Black Religion.* Minneapolis: Augsburg Fortress, 1990.

Walker, Wyatt Tee. *Somebody's Calling My Name: Black Sacred Music and Social Change.* Valley Forge: Judson Press, 1979.

Westermeyer, Paul. *Te Deum: The Church and Music.* Minneapolis: Augsburg Fortress, 1998.

________. *The Church Musician.* Minneapolis: Augsburg Fortress, 1997.

———. *The Heart of the Matter*. Chicago: GIA Publications, 2001.

Wilson-Dickson, Andrew. *The Story of Christian Music*. Minneapolis: Augsburg Fortress, 2003.

Introduction

Brand, Eugene L. *Baptism: A Pastoral Perspective*. Minneapolis: Augsburg Fortress, 1975.

Marty, Martin. *Baptism*. Minneapolis: Augsburg Fortress, 1962.

Ramshaw, Elaine. *Ritual and Pastoral Care*. Minneapolis: Augsburg Fortress, 1987.

Trigg, Jonathan D. *Baptism in the Theology of Martin Luther*. Boston: Brill Academic Publishers, 2001.

Willimon, William H. *Worship as Pastoral Care*. Nashville: Abingdon Press, 1979.

Chapter one & Chapter two

Bone, David L. and Mary J. Scifres. *Prepare—A Weekly Worship Planbook for Pastors and Musicians*. Nashville: Abingdon Press, annual.

Groome, Thomas H. *Language for a "Catholic" Church*. Kansas City: Sheed and Ward, 1991.

Hardesty, Nancy A. *Inclusive Language in the Church*. Atlanta: John Knox Press, 1987.

Indexes for Worship Planning. Minneapolis: Augsburg Fortress, 1996.

Leading the Church's Song. Minneapolis: Augsburg Fortress, 1998.

Lift Up Your Hearts: ELCIC Resources and Ecumenical Helps for Liturgy, Worship, and Spirituality. www.worship.ca/sec3.html

Mitchell, Robert H. *I Don't Like that Music*. Carol Stream, Ill.: Hope Publishing Company, 1993.

The Music Ministry Organization Kit (CD-ROM). www.lighthousemusicworks.com

Music Planning. www.augsburgfortress.org/store/itemseries.asp?CLSID=68966

Ramshaw, Gail. *Reviving Sacred Speech: The Meaning of Liturgical Language.* Akron: OSL Publications, 2000.

Sundays and Seasons. Minneapolis: Augsburg Fortress, annual.

Wren, Brian. *What Language Shall I Borrow? God-Talk in Worship: A Male Response to Feminist Theology*. New York: Crossroad Publishing Company, 1990.

Chapter three

Bertalot, John. *John Bertalot's Immediately Practical Tips for Choral Directors.* Minneapolis: Augsburg Fortress, 1994.

Devinney, Richard. *The Wednesday Workout: Practical Techniques for Rehearsing the Church Choir.* Nashville: Abingdon Press, 1993.

Haasemann, Frauke, and James M. Jordan. *Group Vocal Technique: the Vocalise Cards*. Chapel Hill, N.C.: Hinshaw Music, Inc., 1992.

Pfautsch, Lloyd. *Choral Therapy: Techniques and Exercises for the Church Choir*. Nashville: Abingdon Press, 1994.

Willets, Sandra. *Beyond the Downbeat: Choral Rehearsal Skills and Techniques*. Nashville: Abingdon Press, 2000.

________. *Upbeat Downbeat: Basic Conducting Patterns and Techniques.* Nashville: Abingdon Press, 1993.

Yarrington, John. *Somebody's Got My Robe: A Lighthearted Look at Choir Directing*. Nashville: Abingdon Press, 1997.

Chapter four

Alfred's Essentials of Music Theory (Books Software, Games). Los Angeles: Alfred Publishing Company, 1998.

Arkis, Stanley, and Herman Schuckman. *An Introduction to Sight Singing: A Structured Approach to Reading Music*. New York: Carl Fischer, 1967.

Bertalot, John. *Five Wheels to Successful Sight-Singing: A Practical Approach to Teach Children (and Adults) to Read Music.* Minneapolis: Augsburg Fortress, 1993.

Eskew, Harry, and Hugh T. McElrath. *Sing with Understanding: An Introduction to Christian Hymnody.* Nashville: Church Street Press, 1995.

Feldstein, Sandy. *Practical Theory: A Self-Instruction Music Theory Course*. Los Angeles: Alfred Publishing Company, 1982.

Jones, Cheslyn et al. *The Study of Liturgy*. New York: Oxford University Press, 1992.

Levenson, Thomas. *Measure for Measure: A Musical History of Science*. New York: Simon & Schuster, 1994.

Osbeck, Kenneth W. *Pocket Guide for the Church Choir Member*. Grand Rapids: Kregel Publications, 1998.

Peters, Charles S. and Paul Yoder. *Master Theory.* 6 vols. San Diego: Neil A. Kjos Music Company, 1963–2001.

Pfatteicher, Philip H. *A Dictionary of Liturgical Terms.* Philadelphia: Trinity Press International, 1991.

_______. *The School of the Church: Worship and Christian Formation*. Valley Forge: Trinity Press International, 1995.

Reynolds, William J., Milburn Price, and David W. Music. *A Survey of Christian Hymnody.* Carol Stream, Ill.: Hope Publishing Company, 1999.

Schalk, Carl F. *God's Song in a New Land: Lutheran Hymnals in America*. St. Louis: Concordia Publishing House, 1995.

_______. *Praising God in Song: An Introduction to Christian Hymnody for Congregational Study*. St. Louis: Concordia Publishing House, 1993.

Scruton, Roger. *The Aesthetics of Music*. New York: Oxford University Press, 1999.

Sing the Faith Bible Study. Various titles. Minneapolis: Augsburg Fortress, 2002.

Storr, Anthony. *Music and the Mind*. New York: The Free Press, 1992.

White, James F. *Introduction to Christian Worship, Third Edition*. Nashville: Abingdon Press, 2000.

Chapter five

Are, Thomas L. *Please Don't Ask Me to Sing in the Choir: One Minute Reflections for the Church Choir*. Carol Stream, Ill.: Hope Publishing House, 1985.

Cherwien, Susan Palo. *Crossings: Meditations for Worship*. Fenton, Mo.: MorningStar Music Publishers, 2003.

Dillard, Annie. *Holy the Firm*. New York: Harper & Row, 1977.

A Sourcebook about Music. Chicago: Liturgy Training Publications, 1997.

Haas, David. *With Every Note I Sing: Prayers for Music Ministers and Those Who Love to Sing*. Chicago: GIA Publications, 1995.

Hook, M. Anne Burnette. *Grace Notes: Spirituality and the Choir*. Nashville: Discipleship Resources, 1998.

Hunt, Jeanne. *Choir Prayers*. Washington, D. C.: The Pastoral Press, 1986.

Jones, Arthur C. *Wade in the Water: the Wisdom of the Spirituals*. Maryknoll, N.Y.: Orbis Books, 1993.

Jordan, James. *The Musician's Soul*. Chicago: GIA Publications, 1999.

Newberg, Andrew. *Why God Won't Go Away*. New York: Ballantine Books, 2001.

Osbeck, Kenneth W. *Devotional Warm-ups for the Church Choir.* Grand Rapids: Kregel Publications, 1985.

Pfatteicher, Philip H. *Liturgical Spirituality*. Valley Forge, Pa.: Trinity Press International, 1997.

Ramshaw, Gail. *A Metaphorical God: An Abecedary of Images for God*. Chicago: Liturgy Training Publications, 1995.

_______. *Treasures Old and New: Images in the Lectionary*. Minneapolis: Augsburg Fortress, 2002.

_______. *Words around the Fire*. Chicago: Liturgy Training Publications, 1990.

_______. *Words around the Font*. Chicago: Liturgy Training Publications, 1995.

_______. *Words around the Table.* Chicago: Liturgy Training Publications, 1991.

Roth, Nancy L. *A Closer Walk: Meditating on Hymns for Year A*. New York: Church Publishing, Inc., 1998.

_______. *Awake, My Soul: Meditating on Hymns for Year B.* New York: Church Publishing, Inc., 2000.

_______. *New Every Morning: Meditating on Hymns for Year C.* New York: Church Publishing, Inc., 2000.

_______. *Meditations for Choir Members*. Atlanta: Morehouse Publishing, 1999.

Saliers, Donald E. *Worship and Spirituality*. Philadelphia: The Westminster Press, 1984.

Smylie, James H. *Between Warm-up & Worship: Prayers for Choirs on the Run*. Edited by Mary Nelson Keithahn. Nashville: Abingdon Press, 1998.

Wold, Wayne L. *Tune My Heart to Sing: Devotions for Choirs Based on the Revised Common Lectionary*. Minneapolis: Augsburg Fortress, 1997.

York, Terry. *Rehearsing the Soul: 52 Devotions for the Church Choir*. Nashville: Abingdon Press, 1999.

Chapter six

Don't be looking here for something to *read* about it! That's exactly the point of this small chapter. Just do it!

Chapter seven

Haugk, Kenneth C. *Antagonists in the Church: How to Identify and Deal with Destructive Conflict*. Minneapolis: Augsburg Fortress, 1988.

Rosen, Mark I. *Thank You for Being Such a Pain: Spiritual Guidance for Dealing With Difficult People*. New York: Three Rivers Press, 1999.

Chapter eight

Buechner, Frederick. *Listening to Your Life*. New York: Harper Collins, 1992.

Coleman, Gerald Patrick. *How Can I Keep from Singing?: Conversations in Renewal for the Church's Musicians*. St. Louis: Concordia Publishing House, 1991.

Goldsmith, Malcolm. *Knowing Me, Knowing God*. Nashville: Abingdon Press, 1997.

Living Voice of the Gospel: Dimensions in Wholeness for the Church Musician. St. Louis: Concordia Publishing House, 1996.

Nachmanovitch, Stephen. *Free Play: The Power of Improvisation in Life and the Arts*. New York: Tarcher Putnam, 1990.

Twenty-five Ways to Become a Better Church Musician. www.selahpub.com/Ebook.html

Afterword

Mahan, Brian J., and Robert Coles. *Forgetting Ourselves on Purpose: Vocation and the Ethics of Ambition.* San Francisco: Jossey-Bass Publishers, 2002.

Palmer, Parker J. *Let Your Life Speak: Listening for the Voice of Vocation*. San Francisco: Jossey-Bass Publishers, 1999.

Veith, Gene Edward, Jr. *God at Work: Your Christian Vocation in All of Life*. Wheaton, Ill.: Crossway Books, 2002.

Organizations and journals

Denominational

Association of Anglican Musicians (AAM)
Communication Office
28 Ashton Road, Fort Mitchell, KY 41017
www.anglicanmusicians.org

Leadership Program for Musicians Serving Small Congregations (LPM)
(703) 250-6757
www.lpm-online.org
(sponsored jointly by the Evangelical Lutheran Church in America and the Episcopal Church in the USA)

The Association of Disciple Musicians (ADM)
Division of Homeland Ministries
P.O. Box 1986, Indianapolis, IN 46206-1986
(888) 346-2631
www.adm-doc.org

The Association of Lutheran Church Musicians (ALCM)
P. O. Box 6064, Ellicott City, MD 21042-0064
(800) 624-2526
www.alcm.org

The Fellowship of American Baptist Musicians (FABM)
www.fabm.com/default.htm

The Presbyterian Association of Musicians (PAM)
100 Witherspoon Street, Louisville, KY 40202-1396
(888) 728-7228 ext. 5288
www.horeb.pcusa.org/pam

The Fellowship of United Methodists in Music and Worship Arts (FUMMWA)
P. O. Box 24787, Nashville, TN 37202-4787
(800) 952-8977
hometown.aol.com/fummwa/index.htm

The National Association of Pastoral Musicians (NAPM)
962 Wayne Avenue, Suite 210, Silver Spring, MD 20910-4461
(240) 247-3000
www.npm.org

Renewing Worship in the ELCA
www.renewingworship.org

United Church of Christ (UCC)
Musicians National Network, Inc.
700 Prospect Ave., Cleveland OH 44115
(216) 736-3870
www.ucc.org/musicarts

Inter-denominational Organizations and Publications

The American Guild of Organists (AGO)
475 Riverside Drive, Suite 1260, New York, NY 10115
(215) 870-2310
www.agohq.org

Choristers Guild
2834 West Kingsley Road, Garland, TX 75041-2498
(972) 271-1521
www.choristersguild.org

Choir and Organ
Orpheus Publications, Subscriptions Department
200 Renfield Street, Glasgow, G2 3PR, UK
www.choirandorgan.com

Creator Magazine
PO Box 480, Healdsburg, CA 95448
(800) 777-6713
www.creatormagazine.com

The Hymn Society in the United States and Canada (HSA)
745 Commonwealth Ave., Boston, MA 02215-1401
(800) 843-4966
www.thehymnsociety.org

The Diapason
Scranton Gillette Publications, Inc.
380 E. Northwest Highway, Suite 200
Des Plaines, IL 60016-2282
(847) 391-1000
www.thediapason.com

Reformed Worship
2850 Kalamazoo Ave SE, Grand Rapids, MI 49546
(800) 777-7270
www.reformedworship.org

The Liturgical Conference, Inc.
415 Michigan Avenue NE, Suite 65
Washington, D. C. 20017-1518